NORWAY

Martin Gostelow

JPM Publications

Contents

▌*Photo p. 1: Lofoten Islands*

This Way Norway

Land of Fjords

Ice Age glaciers shaped Norway, especially its unrivalled fjords. Other nations with long sea inlets use the same Norse word for them, but Norway's are the best-known, the deepest and most beautiful. And the ice is still at work: Europe's biggest glaciers cover high mountain ranges and fan out along the valleys, their multiple tongues tipped by cloudy blue lakes of melt-water and the rocks and debris left behind by their gradual retreat.

So for the traveller, Norway is an awe-inspiring spectacle. Ships can sail 160 km (100 miles) up some of the fjords, between precipitous cliffs topped by tiny farms. Mountain peaks to rival the Alps form a white wall—the snow lingers well into summer.

Facts and Figures

The Norwegians are fiercely patriotic, perhaps because they were denied their independence for so long. And these 4 million people have much to be proud of. Their narrow strip of land facing the North Atlantic boasts some of the most magnificent scenery in the world. Longer than any other country in Europe, it measures 2,800 km (1,740 miles) from top to bottom, not counting remote Svalbard in the Arctic Sea. An impressive statistic, but the coastline is so convoluted that if you could walk all of its sea perimeter you would clock up an amazing 23,000 km (14,000 miles). And that's not counting an estimated 150,000 islands and islets.

The Cities

Oslo is the quietest of the Scandinavian capitals, but there's a lot to see, from Viking ships to exciting art. And like the rest of the country, it's clean, uncrowded and prosperous. Bright, colourful Stavanger buzzes with activity as the headquarters of the offshore oil industry. Bergen, the ancient capital and Hanseatic trading port, shares some of the oil action, and welcomes a host of visitors on their way to the fjords. Many of them just drop in on an excursion from a cruise ship, and it's a measure of the trust inspired by Norway's seafarers that most of the world's luxury cruise liners have Norwegian officers on the bridge.

Along the Coast

Protected from the Atlantic by islands, or hidden at the head of their own fjords, picturesque

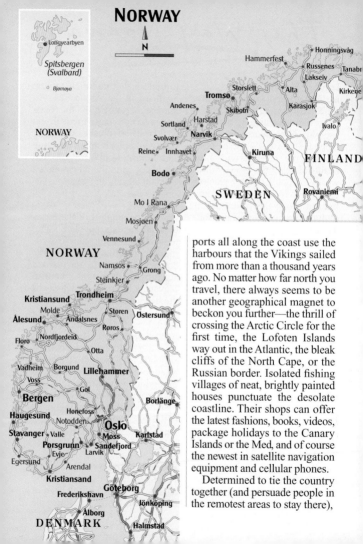

NORRWAY

N

ports all along the coast use the harbours that the Vikings sailed from more than a thousand years ago. No matter how far north you travel, there always seems to be another geographical magnet to beckon you further—the thrill of crossing the Arctic Circle for the first time, the Lofoten Islands way out in the Atlantic, the bleak cliffs of the North Cape, or the Russian border. Isolated fishing villages of neat, brightly painted houses punctuate the desolate coastline. Their shops can offer the latest fashions, books, videos, package holidays to the Canary Islands or the Med, and of course the newest in satellite navigation equipment and cellular phones.

Determined to tie the country together (and persuade people in the remotest areas to stay there), the government has spent vast sums on infrastructure, especially in the north. Bridges or tunnels link almost every significant island to its neighbours or to the mainland. Each little port or settlement, no matter how far-flung, has its connection to the highway system, and great efforts are made to keep the roads open. While many mountain passes are blocked by winter snow, increasing numbers of tunnels provide alternative routes. And even some places officially rated as villages have airports and daily flights.

The comfortable way to see the coast and islands is from the ships of the Coastal Express (see p. 33). On land, the ribbon of road threads through a wilderness of rock and moorland, snow-covered until spring, marshy when the thaw comes and the source of a plague of mosquitoes. Herded by the indigenous Sami people, reindeer graze the multicoloured carpet of lichens and mosses, heathers and cloudberries and bright patches of summer grass.

Towns and villages compete for the title of "most northerly", but the prize has to go to Svalbard (or Spitsbergen), the island group halfway between the top end of mainland Norway and the North Pole, where polar bears roam and the midnight sun lasts for four months.

Midwinter darkness isn't pitch black, in spite of the jokey postcards sold in Arctic souvenir shops. The moon and stars seem supernaturally bright, illuminating snow-covered mountains and plains in a ghostly glow. On a clear night there's a good chance of seeing the far north's eeriest spectacle, the Northern Lights dancing across the heavens.

THANKS TO THE GULF STREAM

If it were not for the warm water that flows from the Caribbean and across the Atlantic at the rate of 25 million cu m (33 million cu yd) per *second*, Norway's fjords would be frozen for most of the year. Agriculture would be impossible, fishing would scarcely have developed and the coast would be virtually unpopulated.

The Gulf Stream exerts its benign influence even way up in the Arctic, flowing past the North Cape to Kirkenes, though in a hard winter, ice sometimes forms in the town's almost landlocked harbour. Rounding the Kola Peninsula, where the Soviet Navy kept many of its nuclear submarines (and the Russian Navy still has some), the last gasp of this great ocean current keeps ports as far as Murmansk ice-free all year.

Flashback

Early Times

The remains of Stone Age houses show that the first humans were already living in Norway more than 10,000 years ago, hunting seals and reindeer. Some settlements were at the northernmost points of Europe, beside the bays and fjords facing the Arctic Sea. As the climate turned warmer and glaciers retreated, tribes of hunters moved into southern Norway from the east and migrated up the coast. Eventually they abandoned the nomadic life and began to farm the limited areas of fertile land. Further north where agriculture was impossible, the abundance of fish tempted them to put up with the harsh conditions; the same reason keeps their hardy successors there today.

Stone tools and weapons were succeeded by improved bronze ones, but the way of life changed little. The small, isolated communities were self-sufficient, fighting when necessary to defend their valley, island or fishing village against predatory neighbours. Then, during the first few centuries AD—the Iron Age in these parts—powerful chieftains imposed their rule over larger territories, turning the country into a patchwork of separate kingdoms.

Vikings

In this land of mountains, fjords and countless islands, it was always easier to get around by water than on land, and Norwegians became the world's most skilful sailors—an attribute that still holds. Around the year 800, the Viking era began. In shallow, pointed ships propelled by sails and oars, Scandinavian raiders ranged the coasts and rivers of Europe, looting monasteries and towns, seizing slaves, burning everything that lay in their path.

What caused this sudden eruption? Overpopulation, worsened by bad harvests? Developments in shipbuilding and navigation? Perhaps above all it was the discovery that there were easy pickings to be had. Many of Europe's religious foundations were immensely rich, and some stood conveniently on isolated islands, waiting like lambs for the slaughter. And towns frequently paid up without a fight to be left in peace: naturally the rapacious Vikings returned for more.

Røldal's stave church, built of upright timber, dates from the early 13th century.

To the victims, it hardly mattered where their tormentors came from, but in fact Vikings from different parts of Scandinavia specialized in different areas. The Norwegians, or Norsemen, raided the Orkney Islands, the Hebrides, Ireland and northwest England. Their fleets established bases, and settlers followed to farm the captured land. Iceland and Greenland were discovered and settled by Norwegians. Pioneers reached North America by the year 1000, though any settlements they established there seem to have been short-lived. The impact of the Vikings was not all malign; they opened trade routes and spread their knowledge of metallurgy and other crafts. European literature was influenced by their story form, the Saga, and Irish art by Viking designs.

The era of pillage and conquest ended in the 11th century. It was no coincidence that this was the time when Norway was being converted to Christianity; church leaders put pressure on chieftains to give up their violent ways.

Unity and Christianity

The nation was temporarily unified under Harald Fairhair when he subdued all opposition in the 10th century. But Norway lost its cohesion when some local leaders accepted Christian teaching and others stuck to the old beliefs. Fierce fighting took place between pagans and Christians.

Olav II had come close to building a single, Christian kingdom when he was killed in battle in 1030. Miracles were observed at his grave in Trondheim, he was declared a saint, and Christianity became the official religion. Nonetheless, turbulent times continued. King Harald Hådråda ("hard ruler") fixed the frontier with Sweden but then invaded England. He was killed in 1066 at Stamford Bridge. The victor in that battle, the Saxon Earl Harold of Wessex, then had to turn south to face the invasion of William the Conqueror, descendant of the Norse Viking leader Rollo.

Under Håkon IV (1217–63), the central government was efficiently organized and Norwegian

1

THE MOST REMARKABLE RELICS

The **Viking Ships** now in their own museum at Bygdøynes, Oslo, are more than 1,100 years old. They can still evoke a chill of fear, a folk memory of the terror induced in their victims by Norsemen marauding in ships like these.

culture flourished. Norway's sovereignty over Iceland and Greenland was reaffirmed. A trade treaty with England brought benefits, and Håkon's son Magnus the Lawmaker ended conflict with Scotland by selling it the Hebrides and Isle of Man, held since Viking days. He brought in German and other Baltic merchants of the Hanseatic League who promoted commerce, although they eventually came to dominate it.

Playing Second Fiddle

A succession of setbacks in the 14th century ended with the loss of Norway's independence for 500 years. The Black Death (bubonic plague) struck in 1349, killing over half the population. Too few people were left to farm the land; the social fabric collapsed.

Accidents of birth and dynastic marriages had already led to a union with Sweden, with Norway inevitably in the junior role. The partnership broke up, but the Norwegian King Håkon VI then married the daughter of the king of Denmark, and their son succeeded to both crowns. Finally in 1397, the Union of Kalmar joined all three Scandinavian countries under one king. Resenting Danish dominance and high-handedness, Sweden broke away in 1523, but Denmark was to retain power in Norway for another three centuries. Danish governors raised taxes which were often spent on Denmark's wars. Norway's possessions were taken over: Iceland and Greenland became Danish colonies; the Orkney and Shetland islands were given to Scotland to settle debts.

The church had been the last vestige of independent Norway, but in 1536 the Protestant Reformation spread from Denmark. Although Norway's bishops met at Bud, near Molde, in a National Council and declared the independence of Catholic Norway, the movement was unstoppable. The Catholic bishops were replaced by Danish Lutherans, Danish became the official language of church and state and Norwegian culture withered.

Christian IV of Denmark and Norway, "the Builder", broke the pattern of exploitation and neglect. Encouraged by the discovery of silver mines at Kongsberg, he spent considerable time in his northern province. Oslo was rebuilt after a fire—and renamed Christiania; the port of Kristiansand was founded; the king paid several visits to the Arctic. Trade had picked up; exports of dried and salted fish to the Catholic countries of southern Europe were booming. In the 18th century, fortunes were made from timber, minerals and shipping. 9

Prehistoric people carved stories in pictures in the rocks near Alta.

Change of Rule

Dragged into the Napoleonic Wars on the French side, and defeated by Britain and Sweden, Denmark was forced to withdraw from Norway in 1814. The Norwegians, joyfully assuming that they were now to be free, adopted a new constitution on 17 May 1814. But hopes were dashed; within a few months they were forced into a new union, this time with Sweden. It was ruled by one of Napoleon's former marshals, Jean-Baptiste Bernadotte, who had been invited to succeed to the Swedish throne as Karl XIV.

Throughout the 19th century Norway struggled to escape from Swedish control. Although the decades of economic depression were not all the result of neglect, life was exceptionally hard. Norway in fact had a good deal of autonomy, but grievances were inevitably directed at the remote government in Stockholm. The example of revolutions elsewhere in Europe added to the unrest.

Emigration was one answer. Beginning as a slow trickle, it turned into mass exodus. Between 1866 and 1875, more than 100,000 Norwegians left for the United States, and in the 50 years leading up to World War I, three-quarters of a million sought a new life overseas. At home, patriotic feelings were heightened by the revival of Norwegian culture, in the writings of Knut Hamsun and Bjørnstjerne Bjørnson, and the music of Edvard Grieg. The dramatist Henrik Ibsen, although he created a national theatre, was out of sympathy with the independence movement, favouring instead an all-Scandinavian unity.

In the 1880s, the Norwegian parliament, the Storting, forced the issue. Until then it had been little more than a talking shop, its resolutions often overruled by the king. But through stubborn insistence, backed by the Norwegian electorate, it wore down Swedish resolve and took on real power. The crisis came on the issues of foreign relations (an exclusively Swedish matter since 1814) and shipping—Norway's lifeblood.

EXPLORERS

In the tradition of the Vikings, the first Europeans to reach Greenland and North America, modern Norway gave the world two of its greatest explorers.

Fridtjof Nansen (1861–1930) took the 800-tonne *Fram*, a tough little wooden ship specially built for the task, into the Arctic in 1893 and deliberately allowed it to be frozen in. He and 12 others spent the winter in the ship and on the ice while, as he had predicted, they were carried for hundreds of kilometres by the shifting ice-cap to within 500 km (300 miles) of the North Pole. Then, with one companion, he set off with dog teams and kayaks, reaching further north than anyone before, and spent another winter on a remote island, living on polar bear and walrus meat. In later life he became a renowned international statesman and humanitarian.

Roald Amundsen (1872–1928) was first mate on the first expedition to winter in the Antarctic, in 1897. His next feat was to sail the Northwest Passage round the top of Canada in a small boat. In 1910, he took Nansen's *Fram* to the Antarctic, and using dog teams led the first expedition to reach the South Pole, ahead of Scott who died on the return journey. In 1926, Amundsen flew in the airship *Norge* over the North Pole. With him was the Italian Umberto Nobile, who returned to the Arctic two years later with the airship *Italia*. Nobile took off in an attempt to reach the pole, but went missing. Amundsen set off from Tromsø on a rescue mission but never returned; his aircraft is presumed to have crashed. Nobile was found by a Russian icebreaker—and lived for another 50 years.

11

A Nation Again

At last, in 1905, the union with Sweden was dissolved, the Norwegian people voting for independence by the staggering margin of 2,000 to 1. The Storting elected Prince Karl of Denmark to the throne as King Haakon VII. In spite of continued emigration to North America, the economy expanded. Norway built the fourth-biggest merchant shipping fleet in the world, but half of it was lost in World War I, even though she stayed neutral.

World War II was to bring far worse disasters. In April 1940, Nazi Germany invaded Norway to ensure supplies of Swedish iron ore by the sea route from Narvik, which Britain had threatened to cut. The king and government retreated to Molde, then to Tromsø and, when it was clear the choice was between flight and capture, escaped to London.

Within two months the whole country was occupied and a puppet regime installed in Oslo under Vidkun Quisling. He was one of the small number of Norwegians to collaborate with the Nazis; his name became a generic term for traitor.

Many Norwegians made the hazardous voyage to Scotland in fishing boats and yachts to fight on the Allied side, along with most of Norway's merchant fleet and navy. They joined in commando raids against targets in their homeland; one on the Lofoten Islands succeeded in rescuing many prisoners. Hydro-electric stations and the aluminium refineries that used their power were blown up, as well as the heavy water plant at Rjukan in Telemark. (Heavy water, used in early atomic reactors, is separated from ordinary water using copious amounts of electricity—hence the location of the plant in Norway.) The occupation forces answered with reprisals, including executions of captured commandos, resistance fighters and those suspected of helping them. Tens of thousands were sent to concentration camps.

The persistent raids persuaded Hitler that the Allies might be planning an invasion of Norway. That belief as well as the active Norwegian resistance movement tied down large German forces in Norway—360,000 when the war ended in May 1945. They had withdrawn from Arctic Norway several months before. Having lost command of the air and sea, they could no longer keep iron ore flowing through Narvik or threaten Allied shipping on the northern route to Russia. In retreating, they destroyed not only port installations and defences but practically every building, a "scorched earth" policy intended to leave behind nothing of use, in case the Russians pursued them. It says a lot for the determination of the returning Norwegians that it was all so rapidly rebuilt after the liberation.

Peace and Prosperity

The Germans surrendered on 7 May 1945, and a month later, five years to the day since he had sailed into exile, King Haakon returned to scenes of jubilation. Quisling and a handful of others were convicted of treason or committing atrocities and shot. Much of the country lay in ruins but so great was the sense of purpose that within four years, production and trade had surpassed pre-war levels.

In 1949, at the height of the Cold War, Norway abandoned her former neutrality and joined NATO, although refusing to allow nuclear weapons to be stationed on her territory. Her peaceable tradition continued, too, in the form of frequent contributions to United Nations peacekeeping forces.

In 1957, Haakon VII died, after a reign of 52 years, to be succeeded by his equally popular son who mounted the throne as King Olav V. He in turn was followed by his son Harald. Norwegians remain fiercely patriotic; National Day, 17 May, is a carnival, with parades in every town and village. All Oslo seems to troop past the royal palace to greet the king and other members of the royal family, who stand for hours waving from the balcony.

The economy was transformed in the 1970s by the discovery of oil under the North Sea, creating a whole new industry and helping to fund a generous welfare system—although the Norwegians still have to pay some of Europe's highest tax rates.

In a referendum in 1972, the people narrowly rejected membership of the European Economic Community. That decision was confirmed in 1994 by an even closer margin against joining the organization in its present form, the European Union.

THE TWO GREATEST GLACIERS

Jostedalsbreen, between the Sognefjord and Nordfjord systems, and **Svartisen** ("Black Ice"), which lies across the Arctic Circle, are vast areas of ice, covering all but the mountain peaks and high ridges. You'll need expert guides and the right boots and clothes if you want to trek across them.

On the Scene

With mountain ranges, glaciers, countless lakes and a magnificent coastline of fjords and islands, Norway can't all be seen in one visit. But with the help of good public transport you can take in some great scenery as well as one or two historic cities in a short stay.

OSLO
City Centre, Frogner Park,
Bygdøynes, Holmenkollen

Norway's clean, bright and spacious capital commands the long Oslofjord, sheltered by wooded hills. It was founded in 1050 during the reign of Harald Hådråda and succeeded Trondheim and Bergen as capital towards the end of the 13th century. After destruction by fire in 1624, the city was rebuilt by order of the energetic King Christian IV of Denmark, and renamed Christiania after him. It remained the provincial capital when sovereignty was transferred to Sweden in 1814. Finally, after a gap of 600 years, it once again became the capital of an independent Norway in 1905, and reverted to the original name of Oslo in 1925.

The interior of Oslo's red-brick City Hall is simply stunning.

Today it's a notably prosperous city of half a million people, though spread over such a large area that it never seems crowded. Cultural offerings include seasons of opera and ballet, concerts by the fine symphony orchestra, jazz in a couple of cellars. The National Theatre concentrates on the classics, headed by Ibsen, but popular productions are staged in a dozen other venues. Hiking and sailing are only minutes away and in winter the nearest ski slopes are within sight of the city. For most visitors the highlights are the museums and galleries, including some unique exhibits in the western suburb of Bygdøy.

City Centre
The central area, which still retains its 17th-century grid pattern of streets, is compact enough

to walk around. Karl Johansgate runs through it from the Central Railway Station in the southeast, uphill past the Parliament and down again past the University to the Royal Palace in the northwest. Hotels, department stores, banks, the cathedral and other sights are strung out along the way, or in the nearby streets.

Domkirke

Oslo Cathedral was completed in 1699. It has been restored more than once, but the baroque pulpit and altar triptych are original. Some of the stained glass windows are by Emmanuel Vigeland, brother of the more famous Gustav.

Historiskmuseet

In its main building on Karl Johansgate, the University of Oslo's museum collections, under the general title of Historiskmuseet, include prehistory, magnificent relics of the Viking era, medieval history, ethnography, and coins and medals.

Kunstindustrimuseet

The Museum of Applied Arts, a little way to the north in St Olavsgate, displays Norwegian and international applied art, design and fashion from the 7th century to the present day. Silver, glass, ceramics and furniture are featured, and textiles including the unique 12th-century Baldishol tapestry, one of the oldest in existence.

Slottet

The Royal Palace , standing in a public park, was built in 1848. It is not open to the public, but the changing of the guard can be seen daily at 1.30 p.m. Every year on 17 May, National Day, marching bands, dancing children and half the population of Oslo parade past its balcony, waving to the Royal Family.

Nasjonalgalleriet

The country's largest and finest collection of pre-1945 art is housed in the imposing National Gallery, behind the University,

THREE RENOWNED ART COLLECTIONS

See Oslo's **Munch Museum** for the first and last word on Norway's legendary painter; the **National Gallery**, also in Oslo, for the broad spectrum of Norwegian and world art; and **Rasmus Meyer's Collection** in Bergen for some of the most striking pictures by Edvard Munch and other Norwegian artists.

opposite the Historical Museum. The emphasis is on Norwegian artists, showcasing the landscapes of Johan Christian Dahl and Erik Werenskiold, the social comment of Harriet Backer and Christian Krohg. The most famous of them, Edvard Munch, is naturally well represented, although the selection here is rather outclassed by the Munch Museum. Works by Van Gogh, Matisse and Cézanne, for example, also stand out in a strong post-Impressionist section.

Rådhuset

Facing the harbour, the City Hall with its twin square towers of red brick is a prominent landmark, begun before and finished after World War II. Its murals and sculptures were contributed by some of Norway's foremost artists of that time. It's worth taking a free guided tour for an explanation of the symbolism, heraldry and history depicted.

Sightseeing cruises of the harbour start from the quay next to the City Hall.

Akershus Slott

The only significant part of medieval Oslo still standing is the Akershus fortress, built on a low hill above the harbour around 1300. In the 17th century, Christian IV modernized it as a Renaissance palace and strengthened it to withstand the new ships' cannon, and indeed it never fell to assault. It was the headquarters of the German occupying forces in World War II: a memorial between the castle and harbour honours 37 members of the resistance who were executed at Akershus. The Norwegian Resistance Museum next to the main castle building records the fight against Nazi occupation.

The Armed Forces Museum in the castle exhibits a comprehensive display of weaponry, tracing Norwegian military history from swords and chain mail to the jet age.

Munchmuseet

A specially built gallery 2 km (just over a mile) northeast of the city centre in Tøyengata houses the vast collection bequeathed to the city of Oslo by the artist Edvard Munch (1863–1944). Of the thousands of paintings, drawings and prints (and six sculptures), only a fraction can be displayed at one time, but they always include some of his most memorable images, such as *The Scream*, *The Vampire* and *The Sick Child*.

Woodcuts, etchings and lithographs take up half the display space, which is all on one floor. Many are based on his paintings, often developing the themes further and employing startlingly different colours.

17

Frogner Park

One of the city's most beautiful green spaces and leisure areas lies about 5 km (3 miles) northwest of the centre. People come to jog, play with their children and walk their dogs, swim in the pool and skate at the ice rink; there is even a Museum of Skating.

Vigelandsanlegget

The park's most famous attraction is a one-man show of over 200 sculptures by Gustav Vigeland (1869–1943), celebrating the human form and life in all its aspects. The centrepiece, a towering granite monolith, depicts scores of writhing, intertwined bodies. The compulsively busy sculptor gave all his works to the city in 1921 in exchange for a studio, paid assistants, living quarters and a salary. The studio, outside the park to the south, is now a museum, Vigelandsmuseet, crammed with his drawings, plans and more sculptures.

Bygdøynes

The wooded Bygdøy peninsula *(nes)* to the west, reached by road or even better by ferry from the City Hall quay, is the site of several unique museums.

Frammuseet

The Fram Museum houses the rugged little ship *Fram*, used by two of Norway's greatest explorers. Sailed by Fridtjof Nansen to the Arctic in 1893–96 and 1898–1902, she was used in the Antarctic by Roald Amundsen, who reached the South Pole in 1911.

Kon-Tikimuseet

The Kon-Tiki Museum houses the famous raft that carried the Norwegian anthropologist Thor Heyerdahl and his crew from Peru to Polynesia in 1947, in an effort to prove that Polynesia's first settlers came from South America. The raft was wrecked on arrival but has been restored. An underwater exhibition gives a vivid impression of the sealife that accompanied the raft's progress. Also on show is the reed-boat *Ra II* which Heyerdahl sailed from Morocco to the Caribbean in 1970.

Sjøfartsmuseet

The Maritime Museum clustered with the other two museums at the tip of the peninsula, is devoted to Norway's seafaring past and present. The *Gjøa*, which Amundsen took through the Northwest Passage, heads the collection of historic vessels and work boats.

Folkemuseet

The Folk Museum, set some way off in a park, preserves over 150 antique buildings from all over Norway, including the Gol Stave church from around 1200. Urban areas from the years 1700 to 1800 have been re-created, colourfully animated by art and craft exhibits, activities and shows.

Viking Ship Museum

The museum (Vikingskipene) houses the world's two best-preserved Viking ships, excavated from 9th-century burial sites along Oslo Fjord, another, unrestored vessel and many smaller finds. The ships have survived because they lay buried in clay, which prevented decay. Now their black timbers stand out against the museum's white walls, their lines both graceful and sinister. The planks of the clinker-built hulls run from prow to stern, which are carved respectively like a serpent's head and tail. Broad in the beam and shallow in draught, the boats could make their way far upriver.

The most elaborately decorated of the three craft, the 9th-century Oseberg Ship, was unearthed in 1904. With a length of 21 m (70 ft), she was probably designed as the ceremonial barge of a chieftain. The precision of the shipbuilders is as remarkable as the artistry of the woodcarvers.

The bigger, less decorative Gokstad Ship looks more seaworthy and businesslike. Indeed a replica was sailed across the Atlantic in 1893 for display at the Chicago World's Fair. The third ship, excavated in 1867, was badly decayed; instead of trying to restore it, the experts decided to put it on show in its damaged state to reveal the inner details of its construction.

The burial sites had all been looted of jewels and armour long before archaeologists recovered the ships, but many other finds are on display. Riding and sailing equipment, cooking and eating utensils, farm tools, a board game and combs convey a picture of everyday life. The wooden sleds carved with writhing snakes and grim faces seem to have been intended for ceremonial use.

Holmenkollen

Only a 15-minute drive or train-ride northwest of the city is a 350-m (1,150-ft) hill, crowned by a famous ski jump used in the 1952 Winter Olympics and every season since. An international event is held every March. Steps and an elevator take you up to the top for a breathtaking view, and a simulator gives an idea of what it would feel like to make a jump.

Skimuseet

Close to the ski jump, the Ski Museum displays equipment from Viking times to the present, as well as some of the gear and clothing taken on expeditions by Nansen and Amundsen.

EXCURSIONS FROM OSLO
Kongsberg, Lake Mjøsa, Oslofjord

Kongsberg

Rich veins of pure silver—not a compound like most ores but the precious metal itself—were discovered in 1623 in the mountains 80 km (50 miles) west of Oslo. King Christian IV of Denmark, overlord of Norway at the time, saw here an opportunity to transform his finances (legend says he found the veins in person). The mining boom which was unleashed was to last almost two centuries. At its height, 5,000 miners were employed to dig out the silver from hundreds of shafts driven into the mountain. A Royal Mint was set up to make silver coinage; it is still operational, but uses humbler metals.

Some of the wooden houses of the mine managers survive in the town centre. Dominating the old main square, Kongsberg Kirke is the biggest and most beautiful baroque church in the country. Built in the 1750s, at the peak of silver production, it could hold thousands. The high officials sat in boxes, women in the ground floor pews, miners and other workers up in the triple-deck balcony. A Mining Museum housed in an old smelting plant explains the history, technology and economics of the now-vanished industry.

The mines themselves are 8 km (5 miles) west of town. The deposits have been long since worked out, but a little train takes visitors through dark, cold tunnels to the old diggings.

Lake Mjøsa

The long and narrow Lake Mjøsa stretches for 90 km (56 miles) like a watery road into the mountains north of Oslo. Many families from the big city have a holiday or weekend home beside it, or keep a sailing boat in one of its marinas. In summer a historic paddle steamer, the *Skibladner*, cruises from town to town along its shores.

Eidsvoll

At the southern tip of the lake, Eidsvoll is hardly more than a village but it has a revered place in Norway's history. Here, on 17 May 1814, following the defeat of Denmark, the 112 prominent citizens of the national council proclaimed a new constitution. Even though the hoped-for independence was not achieved until 1905, Sweden forcing them into a union, the constitution remained in force. The house outside Eidsvoll where it was signed, kept as it was then, is a place of pilgrimage for Norwegians.

Lillehammer

The resort at the northern end of Lake Mjøsa, 170 km (105 miles) from Oslo, is one of the biggest winter sports centres in Scandinavia—it hosted the 1994 Winter Olympics. All bright and new-looking with Swiss chalet-style buildings, it is equally popular in summer for hiking, fishing and all kinds of watersports, or a gentle scenic excursion on the lake.

The Norsk Veimuseum displays every sort of wheeled conveyance, from early bicycles to veteran cars and even recent models, many of them made in Norway.

Maihaugen

The Sandvig Collection of old buildings, started in 1887 by Anders Sandvig, an ailing dentist who regained good health in these mountains, is one of the biggest and best of many such "open-air museums" in Norway. It has 140 examples including working farms with animals and crops, barns, workshops, a fine 13th-century stave church and a variety of houses. Many of them are furnished with original contents, tens of thousands of artefacts and everyday objects from the past. In summer, some traditional crafts are demonstrated—there's even a chance for visitors to try their hand at pottery, spinning and weaving.

Oslofjord

The inlet between Oslo and the sea, 100 km (60 miles) long, may lack the drama of the great fjords of western Norway, but it has charms of its own. There's a string of beaches down both the eastern and western shores, and thousands of small boats are moored in almost every inlet.

Fredrikstad

The modern town on one bank is nothing out of the ordinary, but a short ferry trip to the other shore takes you to the Old Town, one of the best-preserved walled towns in all of Scandinavia. Its fortifications date from the 17th-century wars between Sweden and Denmark. Within the grass-topped stone ramparts, quiet cobblestone streets are lined by the original houses. A museum set up in the former prison fills in the historical background.

Tønsberg

Tønsberg dates its foundation to 871, which would make it one of the oldest towns in Norway. It was important in the Middle Ages, but its fortress was destroyed by the Swedes in 1503 and never rebuilt. The ruins still stand above the modern town. The port became a whaling centre in the 19th century; the County Museum has photographs, equipment and some whale skeletons. 21

SOUTHERN NORWAY

Larvik, Skien, Arendal, Kristiansand, Mandal,
Sola, Sandnes, Stavanger, Karmøy, Haugesund

Larvik

An old port to the west of Oslo-fjord, Larvik was evidently important in the Viking era; more than a hundred burial mounds from that time can be found in the area. It is now the Norwegian end of the busy ferry link with Frederikshavn in Denmark. Larvik Kirke is a 17th-century church with many fine paintings, including one by Lucas Cranach the Elder. In summer, the coast and islands near Larvik are favourites with people from Oslo who come to sail, fish and swim.

Skien

A port and industrial town, the capital of Telemark county, Skien was the birthplace of the great dramatist Henrik Ibsen (1828–1906), author of *A Doll's House* and *Hedda Gabler*. North of town is Venstop, the home where he grew up, preserved as it was in his day.

Skien is the starting point for lake and river cruises. One of the best passes through spectacular mountain scenery to Dalen, at the head of Lake Bandak.

*Prekestolen – Pulpit Rock – towers
vertiginously over the Lysefjord.*

Arendal

Built on seven islands linked by bridges, Arendal grew prosperous in the 17th century from timber exports, an industry which continues today. The town was one of Norway's leading ports during the last days of the great sailing ships and still trains sailors at the Seamen's School.

Most of Arendal was destroyed by fire in the 1860s but several of its picturesque old white-painted wooden houses have survived. So has the imposing Rådhuset (town hall), dating from 1813, one of the country's largest wooden structures. Part of it is now a portrait gallery.

The Aust-Agder Museum at Langsæ covers the region's cultural and maritime history.

Merdøgård, half an hour away by boat on Merdø island, was the home of an 18th-century sea captain and now houses a museum of the sailing ship era.

Grimstad

Like Skien, the small port of Grimstad, 20 km (12 miles) down the coast from Arendal, celebrates its connection with Henrik Ibsen. Young Henrik arrived there in 1843 at the age of 15 to make his way in the world: his 23 father had gone bankrupt. In the Bymuseum you can see the old apothecary shop where he worked as a pharmacist's apprentice, and the room where he lived and wrote his first play, *Catilina*. Ibsen memorabilia are on show, including letters, poems and pictures he painted.

Lillesand

A picture-postcard town of old wooden houses, Lillesand was an important port in the 19th century, with shipyards to build its fleet of timber-carrying ships. The perfect harbour is still its focal point, nowadays for pleasure craft. Beside the marina, gardens filled with roses set the tone for a place proud of its past and anxious to beautify the present. The sea route to Kristiansand passes through a marvellous maze of islands and skerries, many dotted with holiday homes.

Kristiansand

Near the southern tip of Norway, looking across the Skagerrak towards Denmark, Kristiansand was founded by the builder-king Christian IV in 1641: the city centre has kept the grid plan he marked out. Even by Norway's high standards, it's exceptionally neat and tidy. The country's second-largest port, it benefits from a relatively warm and sunny climate which has also made it a

vacation centre, especially for sailing among the hundreds of little islands offshore. Crowds pack the nearby beaches whenever the weather is at all encouraging, and the easy-going atmosphere can sometimes recall the Mediterranean more than Scandinavia.

During World War II, the German occupiers built powerful coastal defences, including the Vara Battery, now the Kristiansand Gun Museum. One of its guns, a 300-tonne monster, could fire an 800-kg (1,760-lb) shell across the Skagerrak halfway to Denmark, where a similar gun covered the other side of the strait.

Tour boats visit several islands along the coast, including Helgøya ("Little Gibraltar") where the Germans excavated tunnels and built elaborate defences against possible Allied landings.

The Old Centre

A square with water on three sides, the compact old part of the city is partly pedestrianized and pleasant for strolling. At its heart, the cathedral was rebuilt in Gothic Revival style in the late 19th century and embellished with the art of that period. It is used for concerts and holds a church music festival in May.

The squat 17th-century Christiansholm Fortress facing the eastern harbour saw action only once, in 1807 against a British naval attack during the Napoleonic Wars. It was turned over to peaceful purposes in 1872 and is now a venue for concerts and art exhibitions. Below its massive walls, the marina is full of colourful craft.

The northeastern quarter of the grid of streets, near the River Otra, contains what is said to be northern Europe's largest concentration of linked (terraced) wooden cottages. Many of the little white houses among the 10 blocks are still lived in, but the district has also blossomed with art galleries and craft studios.

Across the river, the Gimle Estate is the legacy of a prosperous ship owner and merchant. The stately main house is now a cultural museum, while outbuildings deal with natural history.

Vest-Agder Fylkesmuseum
One of Norway's biggest openair museums of traditional buildings can be found at Kongsgård, 5 km (3 miles) east of Kristiansand. Farms, houses and workshops up to 400 years old contain antique furniture, toys, textiles, glass and the household goods of the past.

Kristiansand Dyrepark
A leisure area 10 km (6 miles) east of the city offers a whole variety of experiences including forest trails, a water park, funfair and a miniature village populated by actors. The Zoo and Safari Park are immensely popular with local families; there's a wild Norwegian wolf pack and an indoor re-creation of a tropical rainforest with 2,000 exotic plants and resident chimpanzees, gibbons and lemurs.

Mandal
The most southerly town in the country, with a famous salmonfishing river running through the middle, was the birthplace of the sculptor Gustav Vigeland. The town museum has some of his work, and so does a gallery in the nearby village of Vigeland where he grew up.

Southern Tip
Lindesnes lighthouse marks the southern tip of Norway, 2,518 km (1,565 miles) from North Cape. Hosts of visitors come to see it and collect a certificate, although there's not a lot to see. Great stretches of sand attract sunbathers, and if the sea is too cold, they can swim in heated saltwater pools at the local camp sites.

Flekkefjord
Trade links with Holland made Flekkefjord a significant port in the era of the sailing ships. The upper town, called Hollenderbyen or "Dutch Town", has many 25

Mandal, the southernmost city of Norway, is renowned for its salmon.

pretty wooden, white-painted houses from the 17th and 18th centuries.

South on the coast, Farsund burned down in 1901 and was rebuilt in an engaging combination of Art Nouveau and Swiss-chalet styles.

Sola

Norway's southwest coast has its longest sandy beaches. If only they had a Mediterranean climate to match… Still, sun worshippers turn out whenever they can, and if it's windy, that suits the wind-surfing fanatics who flock to Solastrand (*strand* being Norse for a sweeping stretch of beach).

Just inland, according to the Viking sagas, King Harald Hårfagre (Harald Fairhair) led his followers to victory in the bloody battle of Hafrsfjord in 872. Having thus united Norway, he could keep his oath: he allowed a barber to cut his famous long locks. Three great swords are planted in the mountain as a memorial to the king.

Sandnes

Sandnes stands in a sheltered position at the head of its own arm of the fjord system. They call it "Bicycle Town", and not just because everyone seems to be pedal-pushing; Norway's only bicycle factory is here, started by the Øglænd brothers in 1892. Bricks and pottery used to be another main industry—a brickworks museum explains it all. The Figgjo factory still makes fine china, and it too has a museum. Lakes and fjords offer every sort of water sport; the town has the biggest indoor water park in the country, and sandy ocean beaches are not far away.

Stavanger

This old fishing port which used to rely on sardines and herring has been transformed into a cosmopolitan boom-town by the offshore oil industry. It was sometimes called the city of Bjelland and Kielland, and Stavanger indeed owes a lot to those two worthy citizens: Christian Bjelland who founded its fish-canning industry, and novelist Alexander Kielland who launched it on the literary stage. Now North Sea oil is shaping its future, but the old cathedral city manages to remain faithful to its traditions.

Stavanger was certainly a Viking settlement, but its written history begins around AD 1100. It was the seat of a bishopric with a fine Romanesque cathedral, and later developed as a commercial centre as fishing and shipping flourished. In 1889, Bjelland opened a sardine cannery; the following year nine more of them joined the thriving new industry. The sardine can with a key was invented here; the key is still the city's symbol.

Just in time—for the shoals of sardines and herring were becoming scarce—oil was discovered under the North Sea. In the 1970s, Stavanger became Norway's centre for its exploitation, the headquarters of survey, drilling and supply companies and the base for ships and helicopters serving the offshore rigs and platforms.

PACKED LIKE SARDINES

Sardines brought wealth to Stavanger, but first it took a broom-seller by the name of Bjelland to work out what to do with them. Before his time the little fish found in such abundance were only used as bait. Then Bjelland perfected the preservation process and launched Stavanger's fish-canning industry.

Norwegian sardines are in fact not sardines but sprats, or brisling, members of the same herring family. Since they live by swallowing smaller fish, they must be left in the nets for some days to digest their dinners. Then they are sorted by size, hung up or spread out, smoked and packed by hand into the familiar rectangular tins. Oil and lids are added by machine.

27

Vågen

Stavanger is almost surrounded by water, and Vågen, its perfectly sheltered harbour, is still lined by picturesque wooden houses. A colourful market is held every day except Sunday in Torget (Market Square), at the head of the harbour. Flowers, fruit and vegetables fill one side, fish the other, a lot of them still swimming in giant tanks. Surveying the scene is a statue of the city's chronicler, novelist Alexander Kielland (1849–1906). For a view of the city and harbour, climb the 19th-century Valbergtårnet, used in the old days as a watchtower, especially for fires.

If you have Norwegian ancestors, you may be able to trace your origins at the Norwegian Emigration Centre near the harbour.

Sjøfartsmuseet

The Maritime Museum occupies two old warehouses facing the water. Exhibits deal with every kind of seagoing craft from sailing ships to oil platforms, and the shop sells the sorts of goods that it might have stocked 60 years ago.

Gamle Stavanger

Along the west side of Vågen, more than 150 wooden houses from the 17th and 18th centuries line the cobblestone streets of Old Stavanger. But this is not just a showpiece; people still live here overlooking the harbour.

Hermetikkmuseet

In an old canning factory on Øvre Strandgate, the Cannery Museum traces the history of what was Stavanger's main industry until World War II. On summer Tuesdays and Thursdays you can sample freshly smoked sardines.

Norsk Oljemuseum

On Kjeringholmen, a small island in Stavanger harbour, the Norwegian Petroleum Museum, in a stunning building of gneiss, steel and glass, tells you all you ever wanted to know about North Sea oil and gas. The highlight is a visit of the "offshore installations" where you can experience life and work on board an oil rig.

Domkirke

The imposing church in the city centre was begun in 1125 as an Anglo-Norwegian project under the direction of the Bishop of Winchester. He had been invited by King Sigurd Jorsalfar to establish a bishopric, and the cathedral was dedicated, like Winchester in England, to St Svithun (Swithin).

The wooden houses of old Stavanger, the town that put sardines into the can.

The main nave is a fine example of Romanesque (known in England as Norman); the Gothic choir was added in about 1300 after a fire. Its carved wood baroque pulpit was the work of Andrew Smith, a Scotsman who settled in Stavanger in 1658.

Kongsgård

Next to the cathedral, this was first the bishop's house and later the residence of Danish governors. Now it is the cathedral school. It stands beside the lovely lake of Breiavatnet, a favourite spot for a stroll.

More Museums

Stavanger Museum, at Muségata 16, has exhibits on the region's wildlife, with a separate section on arts and crafts, costumes and furniture.

The Archaeology Museum (Storgate 27) spans the eras from the Stone Age to the medieval monastic period. Among the displays are tools made from bone and horn from Vistehola cave, a site 10 km (6 miles) from Stavanger at Randaberg where humans lived 6,000 years ago.

Rogaland Art Museum (Kunstmuseum) in Mosvanparken has a collection of paintings by Stavanger's Lars Hertervig (1830–1902) as well as a general sampling of works by other Norwegian artists.

Ullandhaug

A pleasant walk or a short bus ride leads to a telecommunications tower with a café and a fine view. The sweeping panorama takes in Stavanger, the fjords to the north and east and the swathe of flat green farmland along the coast to the south. Also at Ullandhaug is a reconstructed farmhouse showing the style of building around the 5th century AD.

Prekestolen

A famous lookout point over the beautiful Lysefjord, this natural stone platform called Pulpit Rock has space for a thousand people to stand on its flat top, with a 600-m (1,970-ft) vertical drop on three sides. It is reached from Tau, a ferry-trip across the fjord from Stavanger. Then there's a connecting bus to a trailhead, followed by a 90-minute trek—not for the unfit or sufferers from vertigo. If you're content to view it from below, take the three-hour boat excursion on the Lysefjord from Stavanger.

Utstein

From Stavanger you can take one of the world's longest and deepest undersea road tunnels, burrowing 6 km (4 miles) through rock as much as 230 m (755 ft) beneath the sea to the island of Rennesøy. On the way, the road surfaces at Mosterøy island, site of the medieval monastery of Utstein. The monks have long since departed, but summer concerts are held in the magnificent church.

Karmøy

The direct route north from Stavanger continues by ferry to Karmøy island. Skudeneshavn, where you disembark, has been voted Norway's prettiest harbour—quite an accolade, considering the competition—and best-preserved old town. Avaldsnes, sheltered by the island, was King Harald Fairhair's estate, and thus can claim to be Norway's first capital. St Olav's Church, dating from around 1250, was restored in 1922; leaning towards it is an ancient, enigmatic granite column called the Virgin Mary's Sewing Needle. Judgment Day, they say, will come when the needle touches the church.

The former copper mine at Visnes was the biggest in the country in the 1870s and provided much of the metal for the skin of the Statue of Liberty.

Haugesund

This west coast port which once relied on herring fishing has taken on a new role—supporting the offshore oil industry. August is the time to visit Haugesund, but make sure you reserve a room: the place is often packed as it hosts the Norwegian Film Festival, a sailing ship regatta, a Sea Fishing Festival and a traditional jazz festival. The Harbour Festival boasts the longest table you have ever seen, covered with every possible sort of herring dish, and the eventful month ends on a bright note with a delightful folk dance festival.

An obelisk at Haraldshaugen north of the town marks the burial mound of Harald Fairhair. Erected in 1872, a thousand years after he unified Norway, it is ringed by 29 smaller stones symbolizing the separate regions brought together to form the nation. The monument became a focus of the 19th-century national movement which was to end Swedish sovereignty and restore independence in 1905.

4 **FOUR VERTIGINOUS VIEWS** Get high on the scenery from the vantage points of **Pulpit Rock** above Lysefjord near Stavanger; **Mount Hangur** reached by cable-car from Voss; **Flydalsjuv** high above Geiranger; and all along the **Trollstigen** (Troll's Ladder) road south of Andalsnes.

31

Every day of the year, at 10.30 p.m., one of the ships of the Norwegian Coastal Express, or *Hurtigruten* ("fast route"), sets sail from Bergen on its way north to the Arctic. The journey to Kirkenes, near the Russian border, and back to Bergen takes 11 days, with calls at 31 other ports, most of them twice. Although some of the stops are made in the middle of the night, clever timing means that ports called at by day from Bergen are called at by night from Kirkenes, and vice versa. At some places, the ship pauses for no longer than it takes to load and unload cargo, while at others it docks long enough for passengers to stretch their legs ashore, and in certain ports the stops last several hours, sufficient for sightseeing or shopping.

The scenes of ever-changing nature from decks, saloons or cabins have earned this the title of "the world's most beautiful voyage". The route includes the westerly, northerly and easterly extremities of mainland Norway, a total of over 4,000 km (2,500 miles). There are only a few stretches of open sea along the way; the ships mostly take an inside passage protected by islands, so it's rarely rough, and the new vessels have stabilizers.

The brainwave of August Kriegsman Gran, the national steamship advisor, the service began in July 1893. The first ship, *Vesteraalen*, sailed between Trondheim and Hammerfest in summer, Trondheim and Tromsø in winter. Rapidly the service became the lifeline of the coast, carrying the mail and vital supplies. People used it as public transport—they still do—but it soon attracted adventurous travellers too. The operators have invested heavily in new, larger ships. With up to 500 berths and bigger cabins, they're more like cruise ships in fact (but without the discos and cabaret entertainment), relying on tourists to make the business viable. The newest ships take up to 50 cars, and some people use them as a ferry, leaving one ship and joining another a day or two later after exploring a region.

The most popular time to go is from May to September, when night becomes day in the Arctic. Fares are much lower in winter, worth considering if you want to see the Northern Lights, and experience the weather in action. Tour guides are on board most of the year, ready with information and busy organizing shore excursions. Some of these are offered at ports where the ship stays for a few hours, others involve journeying by land from one port and meeting the ship again at the next.

BERGEN AND THE WESTERN FJORDS

Bergen, Hardangerfjord, Voss, Sognefjord, Måløy, Nordfjord, Ålesund, Geirangerfjord, Molde, Kristiansund

The beauty of the fjords brought tourism to Norway in the mid-19th century and they are still its greatest attraction. Bergen, well worth a visit in its own right, is the usual starting point for sightseeing trips by land or water. An international airport, a scenic rail route from Oslo and ferries from Britain and Denmark make it easily accessible. Excursion boats also cruise the fjords from Ålesund, Molde, Åndalsnes, Bergen and other ports. Regular ferry services, buses and trains offer other alternatives.

Bergen

Founded as a fishing village in 1070, Bergen, with its perfectly sheltered harbour and access to the Atlantic, soon developed into a trading centre. By the 13th century it was the most important city in Norway and the royal capital, where five kings were crowned. Then Oslo took precedence, but around 1350, Hansa merchants from north German and other ports established themselves in Bergen and dominated

Restored Hansa homes and warehouses line Bergen's Bryggen.

its commerce for several hundred years. Later, under Danish rule, it suffered from discrimination in favour of Copenhagen, but in the 19th and 20th centuries came into its own again. It is now the second city of Norway, with a population of over 220,000.

Until the railway reached Bergen in 1909, it was quicker and easier to get to London than to Oslo. A favourite with seamen, fishermen and travellers from afar, the port was and remains cosmopolitan and dynamic. Its citizens used to claim: "I'm not from Norway, I'm from Bergen".

There's a full cultural calendar: the Bergen International Festival in May and June features concerts, ballet and opera in the glass-sided Grieghallen, named after the city's famous son, the composer Edvard Grieg.

Vågen

Although it can rain 220 days a year, the wooden houses of the old town were frequent victims of fire, but thanks to restoration work the quayside looks much as it might have done in the time of the Hanseatic League. On most summer days, a cruise ship docks at the outer end of the harbour, 35 and every evening of the year the Coastal Express sails from the Puddefjorden quay, along the Norwegian coast bound for the Arctic.

Across the harbour, high speed catamarans wait to whisk you to ports and fjords up and down the coast: Sognefjord, Nordfjord, Hardangerfjord and Stavanger.

Bergenhus

The fortress built to guard the north entrance to the harbour dates from the 12th century. Within its walls, the step-gabled Håkonshallen (Håkon's Hall) served as a wedding and coronation palace for the growing Norwegian empire. The first great event staged there was the marriage in 1261 of King Magnus the Lawmender and Princess Ingeborg of Denmark when, it's said, a thousand guests were invited and the party went on for three days and nights.

The 16th-century Rosenkrantz Tower is named after a powerful governor of Bergen, Erik Rosenkrantz, who recruited a Scottish architect and masons to create a Renaissance castle. By way of grand halls, narrow passages and spiral staircases, you reach the battlemented roof, covered with immense slate slabs. The tower and Håkonshallen were badly damaged in 1944, when a German munitions ship blew up in the harbour, but they have been meticulously restored.

Fiskerimuseet

On the harbourside behind the fortress, the Fishery Museum displays models of old fishing boats, antique knives and nets and huge harpoon guns that were used to spear the great whales.

Mariakirken

St Mary's, begun in the 11th century, is the city's oldest and finest church. Whereas most Bergen churches were destroyed or abandoned at the time of the Reformation, this was the parish church of the Hanseatic merchants and thus protected. An austere exterior gives no clue to the treasures within, reached by way of a fine Romanesque doorway. The magnificent baroque pulpit is adorned with carved and painted figures—including female nudes that must have been a distraction to the merchants' apprentices—and inlaid with tortoiseshell. A magnificently gilded 15th-century North German triptych glows above the altar, while 17th-century statues of saints line the upper walls.

Bryggen

Gabled wooden houses, leaning at odd angles, line the quay along the north side of the harbour. Originally built in the 14th century for the Hanseatic merchants, they suffered fires from time to time: the present structures date from as early as 1702 and as recently as 1956. A modern extension contains shops, art galleries and restaurants, while a modern hotel cleverly imitates the old style.

Bryggens Museum

The imaginative Bryggens Museum shows a wealth of medieval artefacts found in the area, displayed in a basement next to the foundations of some 11th-century houses, excavated after a fire in 1955. Timbers from a large trading vessel, re-used in the houses so long ago, have been assembled again to give an idea of the ship's shape and size.

Schøtstuene

At Øvregaten 50, near the Bryggens Museum, this was the merchants' social club and assembly rooms, and also housed the apprentices' school—equipped with the dual incentives of Bible and cane.

Hanseatisk Museum

The Hanseatic Museum, in an old wooden house near the head of the harbour, depicts the life of the merchants in the 14th century. Young apprentices slept upstairs in little box beds. Conditions were spartan; fear of fire meant there was no heating.

Torget

The market square at the head of the harbour is filled most mornings with a colourful collection of stalls selling a variety of fish but especially salmon—fresh, smoked and dill-marinated gravlaks—together with fruit, vegetables, flowers and some craft goods. Feeling hungry? There's a choice of open smoked salmon sandwiches and filled rolls.

Town Centre

Southwest from Torget, the extra-wide Torgalmenning avenue is lined with shops. A monument in the middle honours Norwegian sailors through the ages; footsore shoppers and sightseers rest on the benches below.

The boulevard called Ole Bulls Plass leads uphill to the 19th-century theatre, Den Nasjonale Scene (National Stage). Bergen is the birthplace of Norwegian drama; until 1850, plays were customarily performed in Danish. In 1852 the aspiring young playwright Henrik Ibsen, then aged 23, was hired as author-producer at the new theatre. Ole Bull, after whom the boulevard is named, was a famous violinist and co-founder of the theatre.

Art Collections

Across Torgalmenningen, to the east, a lake and small park are big attractions for local people when

37

it's fine, to stroll with their children, feed the birds or just sit in the sun.

The Grieghallen and several art collections have their home on the south side of the lake. Rasmus Meyer's Collection, left to the city by a business magnate, focuses on Scandinavian paintings from 1850 to 1914, with over 30 by Edvard Munch including *Girls on the Bridge*. His *Four Ages of Woman*, *Three Stages of Woman*, *Jealousy* and *Melancholy* epitomize the idolatry, lust, jealousy and fear which women seem to have evoked in him. It's intriguing also to see powerful work by some of his contemporaries such as Krohg and Wold-Torne, who are scarcely known outside Norway.

In the same street is the Bergen Museum of Art incorporating another bequest, Stenersen's Art Collection, starring works by Munch, as well as Picasso, Klee, Kandinsky and other 20th-century masters.

More Museums

The University of Bergen, uphill to the south of the city centre, has a botanical garden in its spacious grounds, and two important museums close by.

The Historical Museum has a whole floor devoted to prehistoric Norway, and another with many medieval church altars and treasures. There is also a Viking exhibition.

Next door, the Maritime Museum displays relics and beautiful ship models (ships in bottles, too!) from the Viking era to present-day supertankers.

Akvariet

The Aquarium at the tip of the headland on the south shore of the harbour is northern Europe's biggest. At 11 a.m., 2 p.m. and 6 p.m., it's feeding time for nature's comedians, the penguins and the seals. A transparent tunnel through one of the largest tanks takes you as close as you would want to be to the sharks.

Fløyen and Ulriken

Seven hills surround Bergen on three sides. One of them, Fløyen, is reached by a funicular whose base station is just east of Torget. There's a spectacular view from the top, 319 m (1,050 ft) up, which is the starting point for several woodland walks.

Mount Ulriken is twice as high, with a cable car to carry you to the top. Even if it looks fine when you set out, take a rainproof jacket: the weather can change before you get there.

Gamle Bergen

North of the city, facing Sandviken Harbour at Elsero is a collection of old and restored wooden houses and shops, saved from destruction in redevelopment schemes and moved here. They're furnished in styles from the 18th to the early 20th century, and well-informed guides show how the rich and poor lived and worked.

Fantoft Stavkirke

Far older than anything at Gamle Bergen was a typical 12th-century wooden stave church that stood at the top of a hill on the southern outskirts of Bergen. It had been moved from a village on Sognefjord in 1879, when the parish decided to build a new church. In 1992, disaster struck: the historic stave church burned to ashes. With extraordinary dedication, it has now been rebuilt, with the help of detailed drawings that had been made of the original. Like other early wooden buildings, the complex roof structure continued the Viking traditions, using many of the design features and techniques observed in their long ships, and the same ornaments of dragons' heads and serpents.

Troldhaugen

A wooden house on a hilltop—the dwelling's name means Troll Hill—was the home of the composer Edvard Grieg (1843–1907) from 1885 until his death. About 8 km (5 miles) south of Bergen,

it's a 15-minute bus ride to the hamlet of Hop, then a short walk through the countryside.

The house is furnished as it was in his day; the composer's rimless reading glasses lie next to an open book and his piano is still used for recitals. Down the hillside, the little cabin where he worked overlooks Lake Nordås, and the ashes of Grieg and his wife Nina, an opera singer, are buried in a rockface nearby. The small museum screens an interesting short film in English on the composer's life.

Hardangerfjord

Every major fjord has its fans, but devotees of the complex Hardangerfjord system south of Bergen are among the most passionate. It has something for everyone: glaciers and waterfalls, pastures and orchards, skiing and sailing. But what sets it apart is a proud folk tradition expressed in song and dance, colourful costume and beautiful handicrafts.

Utne

Four arms of the fjord meet at Utne, a village in the shadow of a steep hill and waterfall. The Hardanger Folk Museum displays the folk art of the region in conjunction with a facsimile of a 19th–century farming village.

Across the water from Utne, the busy ferry station of Kinsarvik has a 12th-century church in Norman style and the remains of a Viking boathouse. South of Kinsarvik on the east side of the long, narrow Sørfjord, the resort town of Lofthus was a favourite retreat of Edvard Grieg. Locals say some of his catchiest rhythms reproduce the sounds made by children running past his cabin and clattering sticks against the fence.

Ulvik

To the northeast, Ulvik looks along its own narrow fjord past steep hillsides projecting from left and right. A scenic excursion up a switchback mountain road leads to the holiday centre of Voss.

Voss

Only an hour's journey from Bergen, the lakeside town of Voss is a magnet for skiers in winter and a good base for seeing some of the scenic southern fjords. A stone cross commemorates the conversion of the town to Christianity in the year 1023; the stone church dates from 1277. Another memorial honours an emigrant from Voss who became a famous American football coach, Knut Rockne (1888–1931). Finneloftet, the oldest original wooden structure still standing in Norway, was a medieval banqueting hall.

Mølstertunet Museum

Overlooking the town and lake, the Open-Air Folk Museum is a collection of old wooden farmhouses with authentic furnishings. Buildings on Norwegian farms were divided into "in", the dwelling houses, and "out", occupied by animals, which had to be kept inside for most of the winter. Until the 19th century, farmhouses in the poorer districts had only a hole in the roof to let out the smoke from fires and stoves. Then, when they could afford to, farmers built another house with a chimney and used the old one as a kitchen, brew-house and laundry. For a view of the local scenery, take the cablecar that runs in summer to the top of Mt Hangur at 660 m (2,170 ft).

By Rail to Flåm

The railway linking Bergen and Oslo passes through Voss; Mjølfjell to the east is a small ski resort. From Myrdal, squeezed between hills at an altitude of 866 m (2,840 ft), a little branch line (Flåmsbanen) sets out on an exciting 20-km (12-mile) journey through sublime scenery to Flåm. It drops steeply through tunnels and snow shelters, emerging into a wild green valley. Passing the

Boats of all shapes and sizes cruise the fjords.

mighty Kjosfoss, a waterfall whose spray showers the train with a fine mist, a photo stop lets passengers out to shoot a wet-lensed picture. The line ends at the head of the lovely Aurlands-fjord, part of the Sognefjord system.

Geilo

Situated on the Bergen-Oslo rail-way, Geilo is one of the best-developed winter sports centres in Scandinavia, with over a dozen ski-lifts, 30 downhill slopes and 130 km (80 miles) of cross-coun-try routes. In summer there's bik-ing and hiking, including treks across the Hardanger Plateau National Park. And Geilo makes a good centre for excursions, such as a trip on the Flåm Line.

Sognefjord

Reaching the sea 80 km (50 miles) north of Bergen, Norway's longest fjord is also the deepest. Its cliff faces of layered rock stra-ta are trimmed with lacy water-falls and topped by fields of ice and snow.

About 100 km (60 miles) from the sea, where several branches of the system meet, the shores are dotted with historic villages. At a major intersection, Balestrand looks like a small Swiss lake resort, except for the Viking bur-ial mounds on its western out-skirts.

Across the water, Vangsnes was a favourite holiday haunt of Kaiser Wilhelm II, who spon-sored the huge hilltop statue of an old Norse hero, Fridtjof the Va-liant. South of Vangsnes, the vil-lage of Vik is known for its medieval churches, especially the 12th-century wooden Hopperstad stave church.

Nærøyfjord

As majestic as any of the arms of the Sognefjord, Nærøyfjord branches off to the southwest be-tween mountain walls and water-falls. Sea birds nest on the ledges, goats graze giddy slopes and seals bob in the clear water. At the head of the fjord, Gudvangen used to have a fleet of horse-drawn carriages. Now tour buses meet the cruise ships and ferries to take visitors up the steepest major road in the country. Past the Stalheimfoss waterfalls that pour over a 126-m (413-ft) preci-pice and other stupendous views, the road continues to the resort town and regional centre of Voss.

Fjærlandsfjord and Jostedalsbreen

A narrow and enticing offshoot of the main Sognefjord cuts north through the mountains to Fjær-land, the resort village at the head of the fjord. This is one of the points of departure for tours to the edge of Norway's biggest glacier, the Jostedalsbreen. More intrepid and better equipped explorers can hire guides for expeditions across the ice fields.

The Norwegian Glacier Centre at the foot of the Jostedalsbreen tells you all about glaciers, with models, hands-on experiments, wide-screen films and a mock glacier you can walk through while it creaks and groans and ice water rushes by.

Motorists heading north can take a road tunnel more than 6 km (4 miles) long. Blasted through the mountain under the glacier, it has become a major route linking the Sognefjord and Nordfjord regions.

Lustrafjord

The long, wide and beautiful Lustrafjord stretches north and east from the Sognefjord. At its end, the village of Skjolden is the furthest point that a ship can go on the whole Norwegian fjord system, over 200 km (130 miles) from the open sea. Luster, which gave its name to the fjord, is a small holiday village with a 13th-century stone church, Dale Kirke.

Urnes Stave Church

High above the eastern shore of the Lustrafjord stands the 12th-century Urnes stave church, included on the UNESCO World Heritage List. Its elaborately carved wooden sculptures of writhing, interwoven serpents and dragons inspired similar designs produced in medieval Ireland: examples of the work are thought to have been taken there by Norse settlers or churchmen.

Borgund

A little way down the Lærdal valley, Borgund has another fine stave church, built in about 1150 and restored in the early 20th century. The all-timber construction has five superimposed roofs, with gables ending in the typical dragon's head prows of a Viking ship. Just east of the village, salmon leap up the steps of a fish ladder on their way upstream to spawn.

Måløy

A major fishing centre and port of call for the Coastal Express, Måløy stands on an island at the entrance to Nordfjord. A modern bridge 1,224 m (4,016 ft) long links it to the mainland. In 1941 the town was the scene of house-to-house fighting between Allied commandos and German occupation forces; it had to be completely rebuilt after the war.

Nordfjord

Narrow, multi-armed and often precipitously steep-sided, the Nordfjord system penetrates east from Måløy to the foot of the Jostedalsbreen glacier. Its longest 43 tributary, Innvikfjord, is hemmed in by almost vertical cliffs; little farmhouses are perched on top, perilously close to the edge. The village of Innvik has a church with the most beautiful baroque pulpit in western Norway.

Olden

The resort village of Olden is a good base for excursions to the Briksdalsbreen tongue of the glacier, 23 km (14 miles) by road and then a walk or a ride by pony cart to the glacier lake and foot of the ice mass. Another extension of the glacier, Kjenndalsbreen, is reached from the village of Loen.

Stryn

Like Olden and Loen, the fjord resort of Stryn has its own lake, and for the same reason—the retreating glaciers left barriers of debris across the valleys they had shaped during their advance. Stryn's looks unusually green, due to minerals in the water which come from the massive Jostedal glacier.

Ålesund

Seeming almost to float in the sea, Ålesund is built on three islands linked by bridges. In 1904, most of the centre was destroyed by fire, and the German Kaiser Wilhelm II, who came to the fjords every summer in his imperial yacht, led a drive to rebuild it.

Art Nouveau was all the rage at the time, and the architects seized their chance to create a whole town in the style. There's a superb view of it all from the top of Aksla, a steep hill just to the east of the harbour. On the way up, you'll see a statue of the Norse adventurer Gange Rolv, better known to history as Rollo. He married the daughter of a French king, founded the Duchy of Normandy and was the ancestor of William the Conqueror.

The port stands near the entrance to four great fjords, including Geirangerfjord. Boats take visitors sightseeing and fishing among the islands, where little harbours and sandy coves alternate with soaring cliffs.

Ålesund Museum covers the region's political and natural history as well as the fishing industry, while nearby Sunnmøre open-air museum assembles some 50-odd farm houses and displays vestiges of the Vikingera settlement.

The town's airport is sited on the offshore island of Vigra, the only flat land in the area, and reached by a tunnel.

Geirangerfjord

Long, deep and steep-sided, Geirangerfjord displays all the scenic splendour that made Norway famous. Not surprisingly it's a magnet for cruise ships; an aver-

Rebuilt entirely after a fire in 1904, Ålesund presents a harmonious façade.

age of one a day arrives during summer, ranging up to 80,000 tonnes and carrying as many as 2,300 passengers each.

The spectacle begins out at sea where ships pick up a pilot near the bird sanctuary rock called Runde, 30 km (19 miles) southwest of Ålesund. Home to more than 70 nesting species, it is visited by many more. As many as half a million seabirds can be seen congregated on its cliffs or whirling like snowflakes over the dark water.

Two-thirds of the way along its 170-km (105-mile) length, after the ferry port of Stranda, the fjord divides. The short right-hand branch leads to the pretty village of Hellesylt, where Ibsen was inspired to write *Brand*. The main fjord continues past near-vertical cliffs, waterfalls and tiny farms where livestock and small children have to be tethered to keep them from falling over the edge. They say that the only way to get a cow up here is to bring it in as a calf; nothing larger could be hauled up the giddy tracks.

Waterfalls tumbling from the heights have been given fanciful names: *De Syv Søstre* (the Seven Sisters), *Friaren* (the Suitor—because it looks as if it's proposing to the sisters opposite) and *Brudesløret* (Bridal Veil). At last 45 the narrow channel reaches its end, fortunately widening a little so that the big ships can turn.

Geiranger

Nestling in a lovely green valley, Geiranger village stands at the very tip of the fjord. Launches ferry cruise passengers ashore, and other visitors stay in the hotels and chalets on the hillsides. Tour buses zigzag up to Flydalsjuv, a lookout point high above the town that offers perhaps the most photographed view in Norway; ships in the fjord far down below look like tiny models. Even higher, at 1,500 m (almost 5,000 ft), the summit of Dalsnibba commands an amazing panorama—clouds permitting—of glaciers and the Sunnmøre Alps to the northwest.

The roads here were built more than a century ago to take horse-drawn traffic, including the jaunting cars carrying visitors who arrived by ship in the first wave of tourism to the fjords.

Tystigen is a noted summer ski centre, where it can be sunny enough to ski in a swimsuit. Top-flight professionals use the slopes to train for the coming winter's competitions.

Molde

The south-facing "City of Roses", set amid the mountains and fjords of central Norway, has attracted visitors for over a century. Ibsen spent holidays at Moldegård farm and Kaiser Wilhelm II of Germany came every summer until 1914. Another royal connection: the Luftwaffe flattened most of Molde in 1940, perhaps in the knowledge that it was sheltering King Haakon. A famous photograph shows him and Crown Prince Olav taking cover beneath a birch tree now known as Kongebjerka (King's Birch).

The rebuilt town with its parks and flower gardens is a base for sailing, fishing and hiking, and an international jazz festival takes it over for the last week of July. Twice a day, one of the ships of the Coastal Express ties up at the dockside right in the centre of town.

From the top of nearby Mount Varden, 87 snow-capped peaks can be counted, including those of the Romsdal Alps to the south.

Atlanterhavsveien

The Atlantic Ocean Road north from Molde takes in the picturesque fishing village of Bud, with its fish-drying racks, and the ancient stone burial mounds of Hustad. Hopping from islet to islet by a succession of elegant bridges and causeways, the road finally arrives at Averøy, where you have to board a ferry if you want to continue north.

Romsdalsfjord

Unlike the narrow inlets to the south, Moldefjord and its off-shoot Romsdalsfjord are wide open and vast. Boat excursions visit the little island of Veøy and its medieval church, and cross to Åndalsnes with its surprising fruit orchards. If everything looks bright and new, that's because the old town was destroyed when a British force attempted to defend it against the invading Germans in 1940. The Rauma river here is famous for its big salmon.

Through Troll Country

The dizzying road south from Åndalsnes, called the Troll's Ladder (Trollstigen), is one of Norway's classic driving experiences, climbing by a succession of hairpin turns through breathtaking scenery. At the top, the 1,800-m (5,900-ft) Trollveggen (Troll Wall) is the highest vertical cliff in Europe, a challenge to mountaineers and the ultimate jumping-off point for para-gliders. Trollstigheimen is a base for skiing, spring and summer.

Kristiansund

Traces of Stone Age dwellings dating back as far as 8000 BC have been found in the vicinity, but the busy, picturesque port of Kristiansund was founded only in 1742. Some fine old buildings still survive from that time, but most of the brightly painted houses are replacements for those destroyed in the German invasion of 1940. The town spreads across three islands, linked by bridges, and since 1992 a 5-km (3-mile) tunnel connects it to the mainland. Excursion boats take summer visitors on sightseeing and fishing trips among the fjords and countless islands.

In the 18th century, Kristiansund made its name and fortune from dried, salted cod, *klippfisk* in Norwegian, but known as *bacalhau* in its main markets, Spain and especially Portugal, where it was—and remains—the national dish. Fishing and fish-processing are still important, but the port is also the base for servicing offshore oil and gas fields. *Den Gamle Byen* (The Old Town) preserves the first school and hospital, an old Customs House and original workshops.

Grip

Offshore from Kristiansund, 82 small islands comprise what used to be the municipality of Grip, with a lighthouse, a scattering of storm-battered cottages and a 15th-century stave church. From a population of 400 in the 1960s, numbers fell until now no-one stays all year round. But in summer this fishing paradise comes alive with a full complement of summer residents.

47

TRØNDELAG AND NORDLAND

Trondheim, Røros, Brønnøysund, Svartisen, Bodø, Narvik, Harstad, Lofoten Islands, Vesterålen Islands

Half the length of Norway is taken up by the counties of Trøndelag and Nordland. The first is a land of forests, lakes, farms and the stately former capital, Trondheim. To the north, stretching far above the Arctic Circle, Nordland is a mountainous wilderness interrupted by breezy Bodø and the grim but fascinating iron ore port of Narvik. Offshore lie the rugged Lofoten and Vesterålen Islands with their busy ports and picturesque fishing villages.

Trondheim

The major port and industrial hub of central Norway has a majestic history. It was put on the map when the chiefs of the Trøndelag region defeated all comers on land and sea and unified most of the country in the 9th century. Then called Nidaros ("the mouth of the River Nid"), it was given the status of a city in 997 and became the royal capital. The Christian king Olav II was killed in battle nearby in 1030, and declared a saint when miracles of healing were reported at the site of his tomb. From then until the

Reformation, pilgrims flocked to Trondheim from all over Europe.

King Håkon IV Håkonsson moved the capital to Bergen in 1217, and then Oslo took over, but Norwegian monarchs continued to be crowned in the ancient cathedral, and the tradition was revived in modern times. Nowadays a more modest blessing ceremony is held.

The Protestant Reformation in the 16th century was bad news for the town. Monasteries and churches were sacked, the archbishop fled and pilgrimages stopped. A terrible series of fires swept through the closely packed wooden houses and added to the gloom. After a 1681 fire completed the devastation, Trondheim was rebuilt on the present plan. Lined by brightly painted houses and tall gabled warehouses, its exceptionally wide streets were designed to limit the spread of flames. Now there's a bonus—no traffic problems. In the middle of the vast central square called Torget stands a statue of Olav I in Viking dress, surveying the city he founded.

Down at the harbour, container ships, coastal steamers, cruise ships and fishing boats come and go; the fish market and Maritime

Lofoten landscape dazzles beneath a crystalline sky.

49

Museum are nearby. Ships heading for the open sea pass close by the island of Munkholmen, site of a monastery in the Middle Ages and later a fort, though it failed to deter several Swedish attacks, or the German invaders in 1940.

Nidaros Cathedral

Built between the 12th and 14th centuries, Trondheim's cathedral (it retains the old name of the city) is the most impressive early building in Norway. The oldest part is the transept (1150), in Norman style with round arches and zigzag decoration. The immensely long nave is Gothic. Some of the builders and stonemasons were brought from England, which explains why certain elements of the designs are reminiscent of Canterbury and Lincoln cathedrals. During the long years of decline, the building fell into a sorry state and was heavily restored in the second half of the 19th century. The sculptor Gustav Vigeland, known for his huge one-man show in Oslo, contributed some of the statuary, including striking gargoyles on the south side.

Norway's royal regalia are on display (on summer weekday mornings and Sunday afternoons) in a chapel at the west end of the cathedral. The bejewelled items, including the king's crown, orb and sceptre, were made in Sweden and mainly date from 1818, when Jean-Baptiste Bernadotte ascended to the throne as King Karl Johan of Sweden and Norway.

The well at the east end, 12 m (40 ft) deep, was where medieval pilgrims came to take the holy water. The spring is said to have gushed from the ground at the spot where the body of King (later Saint) Olav was first buried.

Erkebispegården

The former Archbishop's Palace next to the cathedral dates from the 12th century. It was later adapted for use as the Danish governor's residence, and now houses museums of ancient weapons and of the World War II Resistance.

Stiftsgården

One of Scandinavia's biggest wooden houses, on the corner of Dronningensgate and Munkegata, was built during the years 1774–78 for a wealthy and ambitious widow, Cicilie Christine Schøller. According to legend, she was determined to outdo her sister's large mansion, and with this rambling 140-room palace Mrs Schøller seems indeed to have taken the prize. Her grandson sold it to the state in 1800 and it was used as offices and later as the Bank of Norway. Since the 1840s it has been the king's official residence in the city, but the public is usually admitted for tours of its austere, echoing rooms.

The Wharves

More wooden buildings line the river's quays, tall brightly painted warehouses dating originally from the end of the 17th century but much repaired ever since. Right on the water's edge, they could hoist in the cargoes directly from ships tied up alongside by means of the pulley systems still to be seen on some of their eaves. Bybroa, the old town bridge spanning the river, is still in use.

Ringve Museum of Musical History

The 17th-century country manor of Ringve Gård, set in a park 3 km (2 miles) outside the city, houses a collection of 2,000 musical instruments from all over the world, including many from the times of Bach and Mozart, as well as Arabic, Indian and other exotic examples. Specially trained guides, most of them music students, explain the exhibits and play selected instruments for the visitors.

Folk Museum

On the western outskirts of the city, a collection of traditional buildings has been assembled as an open-air museum. The houses both grand and humble, farms, a stave church, fisherman's cottages, are all typical of the Trøndelag region. Many of them contain original furnishings, household goods and crafts illustrating the folklore of Trøndelag. Another section covers the culture of the Sami people.

Røros

Anyone with an interest in industrial archaeology and the time for a two-day excursion from Trondheim shouldn't miss a remarkable copper-mining town deep in the mountains 180 km (110 miles) to the southeast. Declared a world heritage site by UNESCO, it was operational from 1644 until 1986, and preserves many original houses with turf roofs, from miners' cottages to managers' mansions. The impressive 18th-century stone church can seat 1,800 people. An old smelting works has been turned into a Museum of Mining.

Olav's Gruva is a disused mine 14 km (9 miles) to the west, with its machinery intact but now adapted to take visitors on tours 50 m (160 ft) underground.

Brønnøysund

A modern fishing port and a trade centre for many scattered villages and island settlements, Brønnøysund's chief claim to fame is an unusual landmark. Torghatten, 51 the "mountain with a hole through it", stands 8 km (5 miles) away on an island, now joined to the town by a bridge. Coastal Express ships call at the harbour, but don't stay long enough to allow a visit, so unless passengers disembark and wait 24 hours for the next ship, they have to be content with a distant view. Geologists say that the hole—now 112 m (368 ft) above sea level—was pierced by the sea, when the land in these parts was that much lower than it is now. Legend has another explanation: the mountain is the hat thrown by an old king to intercept an arrow fired by the knight Hestmannen at his reluctant lady-love. The hat with its arrowhole is frozen in stone.

Svartisen

Sprawling across the Arctic Circle, Norway's second-largest ice mass covers an area of 370 sq km (145 sq miles). It takes its name Svartisen, meaning "black ice", from the layer of rocks and dirt that has accumulated on parts of its surface. Some 60 glacier tongues jut from it, pierced here and there by pinnacles of rock rising to heights of more than 1,500 m (5,000 ft).

Passengers on some cruise ships and the vessels of the Coastal Express can transfer to a smaller excursion boat to cross Vågsbotn and idyllic Holandsfjord to the foot of one of these tongues of blue ice, formed of snow compressed for up to 2,500

POET AND PRINCESSES

At the southern tip of the island of Alsten, just to the south of the port of Sandnessjøen, lies Alstahaug, a place dear to the hearts of Norwegians. Here lived the poet Petter Dass (originally the Scottish name Dundas), parson of the 12th-century church until his death in 1707. So revered was his work that for a century after he died passing ships would dip their sails. His poems about the Coast Lapp culture are still cherished; a biennial festival is held in celebration.

The little church stands at the foot of one of seven mountain peaks all in a row, about 1,000 m (3,300 ft) high and one of the most striking of the many landmarks that guide sailors in these latitudes. Called the Seven Sisters, they are said to be the daughters of the King of Sulitjelma, characters in the same story as Hestmannen and the king's hat. Like trolls, they failed to hide before the sunrise and were turned to stone. Hestmannen suffered the same fate: he and his horse became Hestmann island, right on the Arctic Circle to the north of Sandnessjoen.

years. Replenished every winter by 10 to 15 m of fresh snow, it creeps down towards its own lake of melt water at 50 to 90 cm per year. Even so, the rate of melting more than balances this progress, and the edge of the ice is now some way from the shore.

Østerdalsisen

Travellers by land can see another part of the Svartisen ice mass. Vehicles turn off the north-south E6 highway at Røssvoll, 12 km (7 miles) north of the town of Mo i Rana, and continue to the bright green Svartisvatnet lake. A boat across the lake and a half-hour's walk over stony ground left by the retreating ice take you to a second lake and the tip of the Østerdalsisen glacier.

Because of its rapid decay—chunks regularly break away and there were disastrous floods until channels were built to divert them—the surface is riven by crevasses and rated as especially dangerous. Visitors usually have to content themselves with viewing from a safe distance.

Grønligrotta

The rocks of the region south of the ice cap date back 400–500 million years and are riddled with caves. The most accessible of them is the sensational Grønligrotta near Mo i Rana. An underground river crashes its way through the network of chambers, and you'll see cataracts and pot-holes ground out by the swirling water and the rocks it carries along.

In a cavern that's called the Chapel, a huge granite block brought there by a glacier sits miles away from the nearest source of granite.

Glomen

Melt water from the Svartisen glacier drives the turbines of a hydroelectric power station at the head of Glomfjord. During World War II, the original station was attacked by Norwegian, British and Canadian commandos who landed from a Free French submarine. They succeeded in putting it out of action—at the cost of most of their own lives. It had rated as a vital target because its electricity was being used in the production of aluminium, essential for Germany's aircraft industry.

A new generating station has been built inside the mountain; over 120 km (75 miles) of tunnels were excavated in the process. The electricity is now mainly used in a nearby factory making ammonium nitrate fertilizer. Using only nitrogen from the air, hydrogen and oxygen from the water, and large amounts of electric power, it produces enough for all of Norway's needs.

53

The fjords and valleys around the Svartisen ice field are hemmed in by steep mountain ridges, crossed by passes which open for only part of the year. Road tunnels up to 8 km (5 miles) long have eliminated some high sections of road and others which used to be cut off by avalanches, but sadly some of the giddiest views have been lost in the process.

Saltstraumen

Twice a day, the incoming tide forces its way through a narrow strait south of Bodø at speeds that can reach 28 knots (32 mph or 52 kph) at full spate, shaking the ground and stirring the air into an eerie wail. And twice a day it rushes out again, not quite as fast. One of the fiercest currents in the world, it creates a violent whirlpool effect, labelled a "maelstrom" (after the original off the Lofoten Islands). And four times a day, at low or high tide, all is calm and still, and ships can pass.

Treacherous as it is, the tide brings in a rich bounty of fish; anglers have caught record-sized halibut and black pollack in the Saltstraumen. A graceful modern bridge spans the 150-m (492-ft) strait and provides a superb vantage point.

Bodø

Just north of the Arctic Circle, Bodø has constant daylight from

THE ARCTIC CIRCLE

What a ghostly thrill this invisible line evokes! To cross it seems to take you into the unknown, a realm of nature at its wildest. Even finding modern cities a long way north of it doesn't dent the feeling, but rather reinforces respect for those who make their homes there.

Ships heading north pass a rocky islet bearing a monument in the shape of a globe, standing right on the line of latitude 66°33'N. On land, the Arctic Circle Centre (open in summer) beside the E6 highway may undermine the magic of the moment, but it contributes a deal of information with exhibits on the plants and animals of the Arctic and the life of its Sami people.

What defines the Arctic Circle and places it at just this latitude? The answer is that this is as far south as you can see the midnight sun at midsummer—or experience a winter day when the sun doesn't come above the horizon. And the latitude of the Circle results, like the seasons, from the tilt of the earth's axis.

May to mid-August and the midnight sun for six weeks in June and July. An old fishing settlement kept ice-free by the Gulf Stream, it is the last station on the northern railway and the administrative centre of Nordland county. It had to be rebuilt after almost total destruction in World War II; the modern cathedral has some fine stained glass and the Nordland Museum focuses on regional history, fishing and the life of the Sami.

The mountain backdrop is spectacular, and the nearby islands are rich in birdlife. Bodø is a base for excursions to the Lofoten Islands, almost 100 km (60 miles) out in the Atlantic. On a clear day, their snow-capped peaks are visible even at this distance, and the setting sun silhouettes them like a jagged wall.

National Aviation Museum

Bodø airport, a hub for flights to the north, is the site of Norway's National Aviation Museum, with examples of original military aircraft spanning almost a century, and a Sopwith Camel simulator to let you experience what a World War I dog-fight might have felt like. One of the exhibits, an American U-2 spy plane, recalls an event that precipitated an international crisis. In 1960, at the height of the Cold War, Francis Gary Powers was on a photographic mission over the Soviet Union heading for Bodø when his high-flying U-2 was hit and he was forced to bale out.

Narvik

Springtime skiers and summer visitors pass through Narvik on their way to the far north or the Lofoten Islands, but the main purpose of the port is the export of iron ore, brought by rail from northern Sweden. Not only is the sea journey much shorter to many world markets, but when the Baltic freezes this is the only economic route.

Narvik fell to the invading Germans in April 1940, but the following month a British and French expeditionary force landed and succeeded in recapturing it after fierce battles in which dozens of ships were sunk in the harbour and the town was severely damaged. Then came the news of the German breakthrough in France, and the Allied forces retreated to their ships and abandoned the Norwegian expedition. The port remained under Nazi occupation until almost the end of World War II.

With a population of about 20,000, the modern town of brightly painted houses and apartment blocks stands on a peninsula between Beisfjord and Rombakfjord. There's a bird's-eye view of the setting from Fagernes 55

This way the North Pole… In Narvik it's easy to get your bearings.

Mountain, reached by a cable car which takes just 13 minutes to soar to a height of 655 m (2,149 ft). Snow lingers on the slopes well into summer; in winter they are taken over by skiers—the runs are floodlit so they can be used on even the darkest days.

Iron Port

Since the railway line opened in 1903, Narvik's business has been to keep the iron ore moving. In terms of tonnage handled, this is one of the world's key ports. It handles ships with a capacity of up to 350,000 tonnes, and as many as 30 trains a day arrive from the mines at Kiruna and Svappavaara in the Swedish Arctic. Tours are arranged daily from June to August; the buses drive among the steep mountains of ore, classified into 15 varieties, where millions of tonnes are stored.

Town Centre

Narvik's experience in World War II was as grim as anywhere in Norway. It has its share of memorials, including Norwegian, French, British, Polish and German war cemeteries, and monuments marking a large prisoner-of-war camp the Germans operated at the end of Beisfjord. A memorial statue in the middle of town depicts not a general or an unknown soldier, but a mother and child, as if to assert that life goes on.

Behind it, the Krigsminne-museum run by the Norwegian Red Cross displays weapons and uniforms, but also improvisations on the home front and in the POW camp. The nearby Ofoten-museum is devoted to the region's history and culture.

Ofoten Line

The iron ore railway, called *Ofot-banen*, runs for 42 km (26 miles) to the Swedish border and continues to the iron mines in Swedish Lappland, linking with the line to Stockholm. Skiers and hikers use it in spring and summer, and it makes a scenic trip for visitors who come in to Narvik by ship. The train climbs slowly through snow sheds and tunnels to a high plateau and then, breaking through the tree line, enters a bleak landscape of rocks and patches of snow. Bjørnfjell is the last station on the Norwegian side of the border; Riksgränsen the first in Sweden.

At the summer resort of Lapplandia, canoes and windsurfers skim the ice-blue (and ice-cold) waters of a lake; a seaplane takes off with anglers and sightseers. The souvenir shop stocks Sami crafts and Swedish glass, and a model mosquito as big as your fist. Only a joke… or is it? Remember your insect repellent on any summer visit to the Arctic.

The Road North

Highway and railway run parallel out of the town, following the Rombakfjord eastward. Soon the routes diverge; the road turns north and crosses a dramatic suspension bridge, high above the fjord. At Trælldal, on the northern shore of the fjord, Route E10 heads east for the Swedish border, crossing it at the same place as the railway.

The E6 continues along the coast to Bjerkvik at the head of Herjangsfjord, the site of a fierce battle in April 1940 when British marines and French Foreign Legion troops fought a larger German force. From here the road heads north out of Narvik's county of Nordland towards Troms, a county of farms and fishing villages, its coast protected by countless islands and skerries. First it follows a surprisingly fertile valley, passing fields of wild flowers and pine forests to Gratangen, 300 m (1,000 ft) up, commanding a superb panorama of mountains and fjords.

Harstad

On the big island of Hinnøy, a stepping stone between the mainland and the Vesterålen islands, Harstad is a busy working port, 57

Fishermen's waterside cabins, rorbuer, *spruced up for summer visitors.*

the home of 23,000 people. When the herring shoals vanished, it switched to shipbuilding and repair, coal-importing from Svalbard and service industries. It recently became the headquarters for oil exploration, which hopes to repeat in the Arctic what earlier discoveries did for southern ports. You'll still see some traditional fish-drying racks, but in the modern town centre, shops sell the latest satellite navigation equipment. Long summer days and some level, fertile land make parts of Hinnøy the world's most northerly area for horticulture, growing vegetables, flowers and strawberries.

Trondenes

A little way north of Harstad, Trondenes is older. Its 13th-century church was built like a fortress; the interior is decorated with early wall paintings.

On a hill above the town, the huge German "Adolf Gun" has been preserved. With a calibre of 42 cm (16.5 in), one of the biggest ever made, it guarded the coastal passage between Narvik and Tromsø.

Lofoten Islands

Jagged peaks, powdered with perpetual snow, rise sheer from the sea off Norway's northwest coast. Entirely within the Arctic

Circle, they form an island chain 120 km (75 miles) long, separated from the mainland by the dark depths of the Vestfjord. When Atlantic storms rage, they bravely bear the brunt, while shipping moves calmly along the inner passage. Even this far north, the Gulf Stream exerts its benign effect. The climate is rated as temperate, which in this context means the thermometer hovers around freezing or just above for the winter months.

Neolithic people arrived after the last Ice Age, and there is evidence of thriving Viking settlements. The Lofotens were settled around 1100 by fisherfolk, and fishing for cod was the main means of support until recent years. Now, the endless summer days bring hikers, mountaineers, campers and anglers by the thousand, as well as birdwatchers: the islands support enormous colonies of seabirds. Artists are attracted by the stunning scenery, seascapes and extraordinary light.

In past centuries the fishermen who came from mainland Norway for the cod season used to sleep in their boats, or hauled them ashore and sheltered under them. Later, they built huts resting partly on the rocky shore and extending on stilts over the water. These *rorbuer*, formerly so spartan, can now be quite luxuriously equipped and are available for rent, but they are so popular in high summer that reservations are essential.

The road link through Narvik, several new bridges and a network of ferries make all the main islands accessible. Fast catamarans and car ferries link the major ports and the Coastal Express calls in at several harbours as well as threading its way through some thrillingly narrow straits. A good road runs the length of the Lofotens from Fiskebøl at the northeastern end of Austvågøy to a village with the engagingly brief name of Å (pronounced "aw" and meaning "stream") on Moskenesøy in the southwest.

Svolvær

The capital and cultural centre of the Lofotens and the neighbouring Vesterålen Islands, Svolvær on Austvågøy is a major fishing port, served by ferries and air services. A library and bookshops are well stocked for the winter nights; other shops sell advanced electronics, fashionable clothes and enticing package holidays in tropical climes.

Vågan church, the wooden "cathedral of the islands", was built a century ago with the winter influx of fishermen in mind. Nearby Kongeskaret (Kings' Pass) bears the signatures of all Norway's recent kings carved in the rock wall.

59

Above the town rise the rocky horns of Svolværgeita (Svolvær Goat), twin peaks so close together that daredevils test their courage by jumping from one to the other.

Kabelvåg

Almost adjoining Svolvær, Kabelvåg is the oldest village in the islands, where the cod fishermen first built *rorbuer* huts. Its church dates from the 12th century. Traces of Viking longhouses in the area suggest even earlier occupation; one of them has been imaginatively re-created.

The Lofoten Museum displays historic fishing and other equipment and some remarkable early photographs of life in the islands during the 19th century.

Henningsvær

The Lofotens' prettiest fishing village spreads over islets joined by breakwaters and linked by two bridges to Austvågøy, the main island. It changes with the seasons: in winter thronged with fishing boats; in summer with vacationers; at other times its 750 residents have it all to themselves.

Vestvågøy

From Lyngvær on Austvågøy the road runs on to the island of Vest-

THE COD RUSH

High season for cod in these waters is January to March, when great shoals migrate southwest from the Barents Sea to spawn. In the old days, almost all of the catch was dried for export as "stockfish" to the Catholic countries of southern Europe. Some still is, but a great deal is frozen, a lot of it ending up as the fish fingers beloved of small children who probably don't think of them as fish at all. No part of the cod is wasted: the roes are canned, the livers yield cod liver oil and the heads and other debris are made into fertilizer or food for farmed salmon.

Catches are smaller these days, but thousands of tonnes are still landed. The preserving process begins with the fish being roughly split, headed and gutted. They are then hung on wooden racks to dry in the wind: the steady winter temperature of 0–3°C in the Lofotens seems to be ideal. After anything up to three months, the fish is as hard as a board, its weight reduced by 80 per cent, and ready to be sorted by size and quality into as many as 14 different categories. Thus preserved, it can last for years. To become soft enough to cook, it needs prolonged soaking and rinsing.

Postcard-pretty, the tiny port of Nusfjord on Vestvågøy island.

vågøy. On the gentler slopes of its western side, the sparse soil yields crops of potatoes, barley and fodder for the dairy cattle that spend most of the year in barns.

Stamsund is a major fishing centre and a Coastal Express port of call. The road continues south, where the charming little village of Ballstad stands at the end of a promontory. At Lilleeidet archaeologists have uncovered traces of early settlers who moved in after the glaciers retreated at the end of the last Ice Age.

Southern Lofotens

The road dives under the sea by way of a tunnel to the island of Flakstadøy, and over a bridge to Moskenesøy. Hamnøy is an ancient village of fishing cabins scattered along the shoreline and pyramidal racks for drying fish.

Å, the last letter of the Norwegian alphabet, is the terse name of the village at the end of the road where some picturesque 19th-century buildings have been set aside as a museum. Ahead, between the southern tip of Moskenesøy and the islet of Mosken, lies the fabled whirlpool known as the Maelstrom. But ornithologists will want to go further, to the rocky islands of Værøy and Røst, the nesting places of millions of seabirds.

Trollfjord

Between the Lofoten and Vesterålen Islands, the narrow Raftsundet strait is one of the scenic highlights of the Coastal Express voyage. Mountains tower on either side of the channel which so twists and turns along its 20-km (12-mile) stretch that at times it seems impossible that there could be a way through. And leading off the Raftsundet is a miniature fjord with all the drama you could wish for, compressed into its 2-km (1.2-mile) length. The entrance is well hidden; ships make a diversion to approach the opening, 100 m (330 ft) wide. They will only enter when the sea is calm, and if there's no danger of avalanches. Once inside, modern ships can use their twin screws and bow thrusters to turn in their own length. Old vessels had to drop an anchor and paddle round using it as a pivot.

Vesterålen Islands

The Lofotens' neighbours to the north are surprisingly different. The contrast starts with their geology: the Vesterålen group is older and more weathered, formed partly of sandstone instead of granite. There's more flat land, some good enough for agriculture but a great part consisting

---

THE MAELSTROM

There are worse whirlpools in the world but the original Maelstrom at the southwestern end of the Lofoten Islands has become a synonym for turbulent and dangerous waters, both real and figurative. Once thought to lead to a subterranean abyss, it was noted on the maps of the Dutch cartographer Mercator in 1595; he may have learned of it from old pilot books. Its name probably comes from the Dutch *malen* (to grind) and *stroom* (current).

The writers Jules Verne and Edgar Allan Poe invested it with more than its fair share of dread. Poe, in his *A Descent into the Maelstrom*, described it as a "smooth, shining and jet-black wall of water, inclined to the horizon at an angle of some 45 degrees, speeding dizzily round and round with a swaying and sweltering motion, and sending forth upon the winds an appalling voice, half shriek, half roar".

This was largely imagination, but the treacherous Maelstrom is not a whirlpool to be taken lightly. When the northwest wind beats against the tide that sweeps between the islands at this point, the Maelstrom boils up in full fury, creating a powerful suction that can be fatal to small boats.

of peat bog and cloudberry marsh. Iron Age burial mounds show that humans were here before the time of the Vikings.

Stokmarknes

The prosperous commercial centre of Hadseløy island is a neat little town of 4,000 people. A short walk from the quayside, the Museum of the Coastal Steamers has models, photographs and histories of all the ships that have operated the *Hurtigruten* since it began in 1893. Stokmarknes was the home port of the Vesterålen Steamship Company, set up by Richard With, the founder of the Coastal Express. As one of the shipping lines merged into OVDS, it still sails the route today.

Sortland

The main town of the Vesterålens was a Viking settlement—it features in the Norse sagas. For centuries, it has been the base of a large fishing fleet, with processing plants to deal with the catch. The Nobel Prize-winning writer Knut Hamsun worked as a servant in the nearby village of Bø in the mid-19th century. Today Sortland is the headquarters of the Norwegian Coast Guard, whose rugged ships and long-range *Orion* aircraft patrol and police the fishing in Norway's vast area of territorial waters in the Atlantic and Barents Seas and around Svalbard.

Risøyhamn

The narrow, shallow channel north between Andøy and Hinnøy islands has to be dredged to allow the Coastal Express ships through—before 1922 they had to sail between Hinnøy and the mainland. Andøy has vast areas of bog, which have become commercially important as a source of peat. Dug out by big machines, it's loaded onto ships at Risøyhamn and carried south for sale to gardeners and horticulturalists as a growing medium.

FIVE FABULOUS FJORDS Picking a few favourites from among so many: **Aurlandsfjord** is a narrow arm of Sognefjord reached by the famous Flåm railway; multi-branched **Nordfjord** is hemmed in by glaciers; **Geirangerfjord** is the cruise ships' choice; **Holandsfjord** is right on the Arctic Circle with views of the Svartisen Glacier; and tiny **Trollfjord** is a hidden treasure in the Lofoten Islands.

THE FAR NORTH

Tromsø, Alta, Hammerfest,
Honningsvåg and North Cape, Vardø,
Kirkenes, Svalbard (Spitsbergen)

Fans of geographical extremities head for the bleak North Cape, "because it's there", but there's much more to see in these northern latitudes. Rugged trawlers set out from a dozen isolated little ports for the world's greatest remaining fishing grounds. The rock carvings at Alta show how long humans have been settled in the area. On the eastern plains, some of the Sami people still herd their reindeer. And the Russian border, so long a most impenetrable part of the Iron Curtain, now sees a steady flow of traffic and commerce.

Tromsø

The big city of the Arctic has two whole months of the midnight sun, paid for by an equal period of winter darkness, but the students attending its large university keep things lively even then. And the world's most northerly brewery doubtless plays its part. The airport is the busiest in northern Norway—daily flights link it to Svalbard (Spitsbergen), halfway to the North Pole.

Gateway to the Arctic,
Tromsø revolves around fish.

Set on an island, with fjords all around, the city is joined to the mainland by a long bridge. Soaring over Tromsø Sound, it was built in 1960 and is still a striking engineering achievement, though traffic across it has grown to such an extent that it is a bottleneck at peak times. Rush hour in the Arctic? Indeed so. Tromsø's population exceeds 50,000 and it sprawls over several islands and a slice of mainland; in fact the city limits enclose 2,500 sq km (960 sq miles). At the mainland end of the bridge, there's a fine view from the Storsteinen mountain, 420 m (1,380 ft) high, reached by cable car.

Arctic Cathedral

At the foot of the slope the 1965 Tromsdal church is a prominent landmark. Sometimes called the Arctic Cathedral, the tent-shaped building of glass, concrete and aluminium has one end entirely taken up by a stained-glass window depicting the Second Coming of Christ.

Town Centre

The official Tromsø Cathedral, across the bridge in the centre of town, is a cream-and-white 65 wooden Gothic revival construction dating from 1861. The fact that this and other attractive old buildings have survived makes the city an appealing exception in Arctic Norway. Everywhere to the north of here was razed to the ground in 1944–45 by the retreating Germans, but much of Tromsø escaped. The pedestrianized main street has many 19th-century shops and houses and an original 1915 Kinematograf still showing films.

Polar Museum

An old warehouse and other early buildings near the port house a Polar Museum recording human activity in the region, with exhibits on the Sami people and the explorers who set off from Tromsø on their Arctic expeditions. The greatest of them all are honoured by statues: Roald Amundsen is shown dressed for the cold near the cathedral; and a bust of Fridtjof Nansen stands at the town end of the bridge.

Polaria

The latest addition to the Tromsø cultural scene is the Polar Environmental Center, in a building that looks like a collapsing pile of ice blocks. This science adventure centre recreates Arctic conditions—howling winds, snow-storms and all—to make it all seem fun.

Tromsø Museum

Run by the university, Tromsø Museum, some 4 km (2.5 miles) south of town through pine woods, is the best of its kind, with departments on the geology, zoology, archaeology, botany, history and modern life of the Arctic. The highlight is the large section on the Sami people. You can see their boats and reindeer sleds, tepee-type summer houses and wooden igloos for winter, utensils of reindeer horn, textiles and festive red clothing.

The archaeology section has some striking exhibits from the Stone Age period, including original rock carvings and tools. From the Viking era come jewels, weapons and the most northerly stone yet found with runic writing. Scientists have monitored the Northern Lights from Tromsø since 1928, and the museum has an exhibition about them.

Alta

At the head of its long fjord, Alta is a busy port, with an airport, 12,000 inhabitants and several small industries. The E6 highway passes through on its tortuous way from Tromsø to Kirkenes.

Ancient Rock Art

In 1973, children playing along the shore of the Altafjord discovered some carvings chipped in shallow outline in the rock surface. Since then more than 3,000 have been found, and many more are presumed to lie beneath the thin layer of soil that covers parts of the rock. The carvings are believed to be the work of the Komsa, a Stone Age people who preceded the Sami in these parts around 10,000 years ago. Simple stick figures, picked out in burnt sienna pigment, show people hunting, herding reindeer, fishing from boats, lovemaking and giving birth.

A boardwalk allows viewing without damage to the surface.

Close by is the Alta Museum, with displays of Komsa artefacts, Sami costumes and an exhibition on World War II in this area. You can learn more about the Sami way of life at the village of Maze.

Kåfjord, on the southern arm of Altafjord, is an old copper mining settlement; its English-style church is one of the oldest in Finnmark county.

Hammerfest

At a latitude of 70°38'N, Hammerfest claims to be the world's most northerly town (although

ARCTIC CONVOYS AND THE *TIRPITZ*

When Germany attacked the Soviet Union in 1941, the only practical way Britain could send aid was by the perilous sea route north of Norway to the Russian port of Murmansk. Convoys of merchant ships with naval escorts were organized, and over the next four years carried tens of thousands of tanks, trucks and aircraft (many of them US-built after the United States entered the war). Losses were enormous—sometimes more than half the ships in a convoy were sunk by German aircraft and submarines based in Norway. The winter weather was often appalling, but the Allied seamen dreaded the summer even more, for its continuous daylight meant they could be under attack round-the-clock.

The German battleship *Tirpitz* also posed a threat to the convoys, but Hitler was so reluctant to risk losing her that she was kept for months in Altafjord and later in a narrow arm of Tromsøfjord, protected by anti-submarine nets and anti-aircraft guns. After surviving minor damage in air raids and an attack using midget submarines, the great ship was at last holed by RAF Lancaster bombers and capsized in November 1944. One of her engines was salvaged by the Norwegians and used to power an electrical generator in the devastated Arctic just after the war.

Norway has another candidate, Longyearbyen much further north on Svalbard-Spitsbergen). Home base for a big fishing fleet, the port's modern look results from rebuilding after destruction in World War II. Three months of constant daylight in summer are compensated by an equal period of winter darkness—the reason Hammerfest, in 1891, was the first town in Europe to have electric street lighting.

Today Hammerfest has a population of around 10,000, a thriving fishing and fish-processing industry, sizeable shops, hotels, even a park with lawns and flowers. The best vantage point for a view of the harbour, or the midnight sun, is Salen hill behind the business district. A steep path leads to the top, passing snow fences designed to prevent avalanches. Reindeer graze on the plateau in summer, occasionally straying down to amble along the streets.

Havøysund

Still further north than Hammerfest, Havøysund is rated as a village, although its high school is large enough to support a big brass and wind band which plays to greet visiting ships on special

NORTHERN LIGHTS

Sometimes they're like waving veils, or clouds of colour spreading across the night sky at incredible speed, sometimes like luminous swords seeming to stab down towards the earth. In shades of green, yellow, even purple, the Northern Lights can be a breathtaking spectacle. Also called by the Latin name *Aurora Borealis*, they are a phenomenon of the Arctic. The Antarctic has its equivalent, the Southern Lights, or *Aurora Australis*.

What causes the Lights, and why do they only occur at high latitudes? High-energy, electrically-charged particles streaming from the sun are excited by the earth's magnetic field, which is most concentrated near the poles. They emit visible radiation, the glow called the Aurora. Although they can sometimes appear much nearer, scientists tell us that the Lights are generated at a height of more than 100 km (60 miles) above the earth. In the Arctic summer, there's no chance to see the Northern Lights; the sky is too bright. The next best thing is to visit the Planetarium on the Tromsø University campus, north of the town centre, where a film of the ever-changing drama of the night sky is projected on a 360° screen.

occasions. Rich fishing grounds attracted the first settlers; now the population numbers 1,500. The promise of offshore gas and oil discoveries, the all-weather highway and twice-daily arrival of the Coastal Express put the little port well and truly on the map.

Honningsvåg and North Cape

The point generally accepted as the northern extremity of Europe is actually on an island, Magerøy, linked to the mainland by undersea road tunnel.

Honningsvåg, with a big sheltered harbour and an airport, is Magerøy's main settlement, still rated as a village although it's home to 3,500 people. Its white wooden church on the hillside was the only building spared in the German "scorched earth" retreat of 1944.

Down at the quayside the small but informative North Cape Museum traces 10,000 years of human activity in this area, with exhibits on the history of fishing and early photographs. Fishing is still the main activity; the port can be jammed with rugged, storm-stained craft from Russia, Portugal, Poland and Britain as well as the local fleet.

Each May, up to 7,000 reindeer are shipped from the mainland in Norwegian army landing craft to graze on the island's sparse vegetation. In September, they and the calves born there have to swim the strait to get back to the snow-covered plains where they spend the winter.

Skarsvåg

The harbour closest to the North Cape belongs to the little fishing village of Skarsvåg, population about 200. The arrival of a cruise ship causes major excitement as hundreds of passengers are ferried ashore. The local children mill about the quay and call greetings in various languages, or shyly offer miniature glass fishing floats or carved driftwood. Sami women sell souvenirs made of reindeer skin or horn, and dolls dressed in the same red costumes as themselves. The hillside behind the village is surprisingly green once the snow has melted, in contrast to the rocky plateau above.

North Cape

Almost as barren as the moon, this bleak, windswept headland 35 km (22 miles) from Honningsvåg gets the credit but in fact isn't the most northerly point of the European land mass. That is on the next big peninsula to the east. But the English navigator Richard Chancellor labelled it North Cape in 1553 and that has been good enough for most travellers ever since. This is where 69

the road ends, dramatically, at the edge of a cliff 307 m (1,007 ft) above the sea.

In spite of the isolation, summer brings plenty of traffic: camper vans, excursion buses and tour groups from cruise ships and the Coastal Express. North Cape Hall, partly blasted out of the rock, provides a sheltered viewing point and houses historical displays, a video show, souvenir shop, post office and restaurant. A tunnel leads to a chapel and gallery in the cliff face, looking down on a sea that one day can be a raging fury, another as smooth as glass.

Out on the plateau itself, the polar wind rarely relents, but in summer a surprising growth of grass and wild flowers covers the shaly soil. A Children's Monument comprises circular sculptures created by seven child artists from around the world and other memorials record royal visits.

The sun doesn't set from mid-May to the end of July, but that is no guarantee that you'll see it. Snow flurries are just as likely, or a chilling fog. Among the seabirds skimming the water, screaming overhead or patrolling the cliffs, you may spot puffins

On top of the world: North Cape monument in the midnight sun.

from the colony of 360,000 nesting pairs based on small islands to the west of the Cape.

Berlevåg

Sheer determination kept the people of Berlevåg in their remote fishing village. There was little shelter for their boats in the harbour, exposing them to Arctic storms. With no pier for the Coastal Express, the people were often cut off from regular contact

ROYAL SIGHTSEERS

The future "Citizen-King" of France, Louis-Philippe, set the trend as early as 1795, arriving incognito at the North Cape and fairly sure that here at least he would be safe from revolutionary assassins. Prince Napoleon, cousin of Emperor Napoleon III, came in 1856. In 1873, King Oscar II of Sweden and Norway made the climb to the clifftop, and in 1891 the German Kaiser Wilhelm II paid a visit during one of his regular summer voyages to Norway. King Rama V of Siam (now Thailand) followed the fashion in 1907 and of course all of Norway's kings since the restoration of independence in 1905 have been diligent travellers to all parts of the country including this remote spot.

with the outside world. Moles were built to break the force of the waves, but they were swept away. At last, in 1970, a new sea wall was constructed, using 15-tonne concrete tetrapods that bind together while allowing some water flow. Now the Coastal Express can call, and the road link to the E6 highway is also kept open all year. With fish-processing plants and ship repair yards, the village is a typical product of Norway's firm intent to provide good communications and employment in the Arctic.

Båtsfjord

Remains of Stone Age dwellings show that humans long ago settled beside the sheltered sea inlet that leads to Båtsfjord. Fishing was the way of life then as now, although today's trawlers with their radar, GPS navigation, echo sounders and powerful engines are a far cry from the methods of even a century ago. Filleting and freezing plants deal with the catch and shipyards keep the boats in good repair. Norway's tallest TV mast, 242 m (794 ft) high, sends its signals right across the north.

Vardø

Here at the easternmost extremity of Norway, you are further east than Istanbul, and so far north that the summer sun doesn't set for 80 days. A short walk from the quayside is Vardøhus fort, with ancient cannon and ramparts in the shape of an eight-pointed star. Dating from 1737, its purpose was to deter Russian incursions. In the same tradition, Vardø's prominent radar domes and masts were built by NATO during the Cold War to watch the movements of Soviet ships and aircraft: the Kola Peninsula to the east bristled with military bases. The town, standing on Vardøy island, is linked to the main harbour and airport by a road tunnel.

Fishing was the reason people settled here 9,000 years ago; it remains the main activity, with big catches of shrimp and cod, and shoals of capelin harvested for oil. Russia and Norway cannot agree on the line dividing their economic zones in the Barents Sea, so there is a vast "grey area". But the opening of the frontier has revived the former *pomor* (barter) trade with Russia which had been stopped since 1917. Now Sami and Russian women in vividly coloured traditional dress come across the border to summer markets, bringing embroidery, lace, wood carvings and other craft goods.

Vadsø

Many of the people of this coast are Finnish-speaking, descended from immigrants who moved in

Trawling through the chilly waters in quest of a catch.

during the 19th century, tempted by the rich stocks of fish in the Arctic seas. More arrived after Finland lost its outlet to the sea at Petsamo in 1940. Finnish is taught along with Norwegian in local schools, and the Sami people of the area study in their own language.

The original settlement was on Vadsøy island, but moved to a more sheltered site on the mainland. It's a port of call for the Coastal Express, although the timetable is unusual; four ships a week put in on the outbound voyage, three on the return. An evocative sight is the mooring mast used by Amundsen's airship *Norge* in 1926 and the ill-fated Italian airship expedition of General Umberto Nobile in 1928.

Kirkenes

Southeast of North Cape is the frontier town of Kirkenes, with a sheltered harbour and a population of 7,000. Vast spoil heaps and rusting buildings on the hillsides are relics of the former main industry, the mining and treatment of iron ore. It became uneconomic and was phased out, finally closing down in 1996. Ship repair has provided some alternative employment, but the main hope is now commerce with Russia across the nearby border. 73

Instead of a few hundred people a year making the crossing, the figure has risen to tens of thousands. The journey from Kirkenes to Murmansk takes four or five hours by bus, rather less in a high speed catamaran.

Very little in Kirkenes dates from pre-World War II. German forces took the town in 1940, and then, massively reinforced, used it as the base for a drive towards the Russian port of Murmansk when Hitler invaded the USSR in 1941. Little ground was gained and the front soon stabilized. During the next three years the Russians repeatedly bombed Kirkenes, which was garrisoned by 70,000 German troops. The destruction became almost total when the retreating Germans blew up or burned what was left. An evocative sight today is Andersgrotta, a cavern tunnelled out of the mountain for use as a bomb shelter; a multi-media show tells of the more than 300 air raids the town suffered.

The Russian Border

Only 15 km (9 miles) from town, Norway's frontier in the far north has scarcely moved since 1307, but the neighbours have changed. This was the Finnish border until 1940 when, as a result of the "Winter War" with the USSR, the Finns lost the port of Petsamo and with it their outlet to the Arctic ocean. After 1945, and especially following Norway's decision to join NATO in 1949, the border was one of the most sensi-

---

LEMMINGS

Almost anywhere in the wild you might catch sight of some small, brown, furry rodents bustling about in the undergrowth or among the moss and lichens. They breed like rabbits, only much faster; at the end of a normal three-year life span, a female lemming could theoretically have over a billion billion billion direct descendants.

Predators usually keep the numbers down, but occasional population explosions occur, sending the lemmings on their famous mass migrations. In Norway, these inevitably lead to the sea, perhaps via a precipitous drop. The sight of a lemming column pouring over a cliff made them a metaphor for blindly following the crowd, even for a collective death wish. But animal behaviourists don't believe that suicide is on their tiny minds, merely the overpowering instinct to get somewhere else. It is not unusual to find a flotilla of lemmings bravely paddling out to sea in the direction of America.

Warmly cocooned, a Sami baby enters into a world where traditions have been carefully preserved.

tive in the world, an interface between the USSR and the West. The Kola peninsula on the Soviet side held the greatest concentration of Soviet forces, especially its huge fleet of nuclear submarines and surface ships and its land-based missiles.

The border takes a sharp triangular bite into Norway, so that the historic Russian Orthodox monastery of Boris Gleb falls within Russia. Its red walls and onion domes can be seen in the distance, on the west bank of the Pasvik river. Since 1992, services have again been held there. A small chapel of the Sami stands nearby in the same Russian area.

Svalbard (Spitsbergen)

No matter how it feels, the North Cape is not the end of the world, or of Norway. Another 800 km (500 miles) further north, scarcely 1,280 km (800 miles) south of the North Pole, lies the island group called Svalbard by the Norwegians, and Spitsbergen (the name of the largest island) by practically everyone else. Tacked onto Svalbard for administrative reasons is an isolated island stuck about halfway between the mainland and Spitsbergen: Bjørnøya (Bear Island), a weather station and bird sanctuary. Cruise ships usually pass close to Bear Island on the way up or going back.

75

A awe-inspiring land of rock and moving ice.

Whalers of many nations used the islands as a base in the 17th and 18th centuries; then came Russian and Norwegian hunters and trappers, pursuing the fur trade. The discovery of coal led to year-round settlement; mining began in 1899. Sovereignty was in dispute until a 1920 treaty awarded the islands to Norway while allowing rights to many other nations. Until recently, the majority of the population was Russian and Ukrainian. Norway and the Soviet Union established mines, but in recent years, production has dropped as the Russians reduced support and the Norwegians cut output.

A last gasp of the Gulf Stream —the North Atlantic Current— explains Spitsbergen's relative accessibility. Most other places at this extreme latitude are locked in the ice, yet weekly supply ships get through to the mining town of Longyearbyen from about May to November. (Cruise ships normally limit their seasons to June, July and August.) The Norwegians who live in Longyearbyen are volunteers who rave about the scenery and the rugged life. They receive tax benefits but few other incentives, yet whenever the local school advertises for a teacher, there are plenty of applicants from mainland Norway.

The presence of the North Atlantic Current makes the western coast of Spitsbergen reasonably liveable. The fog that usually stands near Svalbard is caused by the confluence of the stream of warmish sea with the relentless polar winds.

Nearly two-thirds of the area of Svalbard is covered by glaciers. As in other frozen parts of the world, the glaciers keep moving, slowly advancing or retreating through mountain valleys according to climatic conditions. The trend here in the 20th century was a retreat.

Those mountains cradling the glaciers are steep and rugged, with notoriously sharp peaks along the west coast. The cruel winter temperatures have affected the mountains by cracking many rock surfaces; the lower slopes are covered in the residue.

How cold does it get? The record low in Longyearbyen is so cold it's almost impossible to comprehend: –46°C (–51°F). On the bright side, the highest-ever temperature, on a scorching July day, was 21°C (70°F). The monthly mean temperature in March is –12°C (+10°F); the mean in July is +4°C (+40°F). But in the sun the temperature can climb as high as 30°C (86°F).

The winter is so long and cold because, as the North Pole tilts farther from the sun, daylight dis-

MOVING ICE

Glaciers must be treated with the utmost respect. Level snow can conceal a deep crevasse, and in summer the melt holes can be very deep. The face of a glacier is especially dangerous; as the ice mass moves forward (and melts in warm conditions), chunks can fall off. Never walk on a glacier, or approach its margins, without an expert guide. Climbing schools run classes on rock and ice techniques—details from the Norwegian Mountain Touring Association.

appears for nearly four months—the darker side of the midnight sun syndrome. In the second half of February the sky begins to brighten. The impending dawn stirs new optimism, and in the beginning of March there is always a local festival to celebrate the return of the sun. After nearly four months of utter darkness, it's the least they could do.

Magdalena Bay

A likely first landfall for cruise passengers is a totally uninhabited tongue of land at Magdalena Bay, in the far northwest corner of Spitsbergen. The latitude here is 79° 33' 72" N, and the scenery looks just as far-out as the reading sounds.

FLORA AND FAUNA

The Gulf Stream, again, is the secret ingredient in Svalbard's relative profusion of living things. About 160 species of plants have been noted, from mosses to buttercups, polar dandelions and pale Svalbard poppies. There are even well-protected valleys where dwarf birch grows to a height of several inches. Note: picking flowers is forbidden.

Big colonies of sea birds take advantage of the climate and the good fishing along the west coast of Spitsbergen. More than 100 bird species have made appearances, though only 15 are regular breeders here. Among the standouts: auks, gulls, petrels, ptarmigan, puffins and terns. Birds of prey stay away, since there are no rodents to provide their basic food. Life for the birds, however, is not very relaxed, as gulls attack eggs and fledglings.

Some bird colonies are visible from a considerable distance, thanks to the vegetation flourishing beneath them. All that fertilizer, especially on cliff sides with southern exposure, produces splashes of colour among otherwise dreary rock faces. Mostly it's moss. Visitors are warned to keep away from nesting areas. Protective bird-parents spare no effort to deter any intruder.

There used to be so many polar bears on Svalbard that cruise ships would arrive on safari. In 1963 conservation measures had to be introduced: only one bear per tourist. But the authorities soon realized that the species required more protection. Since 1973, hunting polar bears has been forbidden. The law has saved them from extinction; and in fact, estimates put the polar bear population of Svalbard at around 3,000—almost too much of a good thing. Since 1979, ships' crews have been permitted to carry weapons ashore by way of precaution. It's suggested that a stray polar bear, sighting all those tourists invading his turf, might waddle over for a closer look.

There are two other indigenous land mammals: the arctic fox and the wild Svalbard reindeer (a scaled-down version of a standard Norwegian reindeer). As to sea-goers, there are small ringed seals and about 1000 walruses. Forlandet National Park has the world's most northerly home of the common seal.

In an effort to save Svalbard's wildlife, more than 50 per cent of the land area of the islands has been proclaimed a conservation zone. Three national parks, three nature reserves and fifteen bird sanctuaries add up to more than 35,000 sq km (13,000 sq miles)—six times the size of all the national parks in mainland Norway.

Mini-icebergs loll about as the ship penetrates the fjord, confined between hostile mountains. At first the mountains look as lifeless as slag heaps, but on close inspection some of the crevices reveal patches of moss or lichens. Deep snow fills the valleys, even in midsummer. On all sides are glaciers: some are as smooth as a virgin ski-run; some gently dip into the sea; others are all churned up and end abruptly in a white precipice. The ice cliff at the far end of the fjord is 150 feet high, though it looks a fraction of that height until you become accustomed to the spatial relations in this unfamiliar landscape. It's all so silent and deserted in Magdalena Bay that the sound of the ship's launch puttering an advance pasty towards the shore statles the passengers.

When you are ferried ashore you may well feel like the first adventurer ever to set foot on this rock-strewn peninsula. But earlier cruise-ship tourists, seeking the immortality of the graffiti artist, have left mementoes. And there are more serious but crudely made monuments, and a simple official Norwegian obelisk, dated 1930, commemorating the travellers who stopped here between 1600 and 1750.

Rocks big and small make up the surface of the peninsula. As the visitors clamber over this tricky surface, approaching the mountainside, throngs of distant birds cry out at the summit. Looking more closely at the rocks of myriad shapes and colours, you'll notice there really is life at this end of the world: ferns, grass, minuscule mushrooms, flowers scarcely larger than a pencil-point—even garden weeds thrusting forth from between the stones. Melted ice forms small lakes in the peninsula's scattered depressions; the cold, still surface reflects the glaciers more faithfully than the rippled mirror of the surrounding sea.

As the tenders return passengers to the ship, it's a good time to remember not to miss the boat: Magdalena Bay is about the last port of call where you'd want to be left ashore.

The Ice Barrier

In midsummer the ice barrier extends to within a few miles of the northern coast of Spitsbergen. This is where the Gulf Stream finally runs out of steam.

The ice barrier is tangible enough to show up on the ship's radar long before it can be spotted through binoculars. When the ice becomes visible to the naked eye, it is seen to stretch to the horizon—not a solid mass at this latitude ($80°$) but composed of thousands of ice-cakes in close proximity. A good long-jumper 79 might just be able to make it to the North Pole by leaping from floe to floe.

Some ice-floes are double-deckers, formed when one cake has been washed on top of another. Gulls perch on many floes, and an occasional seal is sighted taking a break on the ice. The fishing is fabulous up here for birds, seals and people alike; you may well sight some big trawlers at work sharing the bounty.

The ice barrier is composed of chunks of frozen brine, not to be confused with icebergs. Mostly found near fjords, icebergs are parts of glaciers which have split off, and they are composed of fresh water. The ice barrier exists because the surface temperature of the Arctic Ocean falls so low for so many months at a time, only slightly relieved by the mild warmth of the summer's midnight sun. Covering an area of about 14 million sq km (5.5 million sq miles), this is rated the world's smallest ocean.

The Western Fjords

Heading south from the ice pack, cruise ships skirt the Spitsbergen coast and take a side trip or two among the western fjords. Each has its own stark beauty.

The Krossfjord divides into two tributaries amidst sharp mountain peaks. The Lilliehook-fjord juts northward with mountains close in on either side of the ship and a vast sweeping glacier at the end of the fjord. Warm weather splits off great slivers and chunks of the glacier, which float off into the fjord and eventually to sea. Some of the resulting icebergs are two or three storeys high. The sister fjord here is called the Möllerfjord. Being separated from the glacier, it is almost completely ice-free in summer, even though it's right around the bend from the Lilliehookfjord.

Ny-Ålesund

To the south, the Kongsfjord leads to Ny-Ålesund, once a coal mining town. It is now a scientific research outpost with a winter population of a couple of dozen. In the distance are the summits of the Tre Kroner (Three Crowns), 1,225 m high (4,000 ft). Ny-Ålesund was the base for several polar expeditions, and you can see the dirigible mast to which pioneer airships were moored—Roald Amundsen's in 1926 and Umberto Nobile's two years later (see p. 11).

Longyearbyen

The biggest fjord in west Spitsbergen, the Isfjord, has a tributary, only twice as long as it is wide, called the Adventfjord. Near the head of this fjord is the Norwegian town of Longyear-

Here and there you'll see a brave patch of green.

byen, site of, among other things, the world's northernmost supermarket.

Svalbard is starting to welcome visitors on a small scale. With new hotels, restaurants and services—and even a campsite—the tourist industry is becoming a significant part of the economy. The brochures can't quite glamorize an unadorned mining town set in a dreary valley between mountains. But there's the adventure of it all, and in winter the snow covers much of the ugliness, and cheering lights shine from every house all the dark day long. The town was founded in 1906 by an American mining en-

gineer and entrepreneur, John Munroe Longyear, of the Arctic Coal Company of Boston. In 1916 he sold out to a Norwegian company, which generously named the place Longyearbyen. (The Norwegian government has since bought a controlling interest in the firm.)

Today the population is over 1,000. The low wooden houses often resemble army barracks though they are spruced up with colourful coats of paint and cheerful flowers in the windows. The residential areas are scattered around the valley, partly to lessen the threat of a catastrophe in case of fire.

POLAR BEARS

Should you chance upon a polar bear, the good news is that it's the smallest of the Arctic bears, weighing in at a mere 300 kg (660 lb). Those that live further west around the Bering Sea can grow to as much as 800 kg (1,760 lb). In summer they eat a dainty diet of berries and birds' eggs, but their staple is seal. With their thick white coats and lumbering gait, they look cute at a distance, but don't take chances. Bears have killed people, one of them just outside Longyearbyen.

Because of the permafrost, which makes the ground rock-hard and ice-cold, the town's water pipes and sewer lines have to be above the ground. This is not conducive to scenic panoramas, marred in any case by all the conveyer belts and cable-car lines to move the coal.

Apart from the heavy trucks which sometimes roar past, there's not much traffic on the 45 km (28 miles) of road in and around Longyearbyen. Most of the locals who own vehicles stick to snowmobiles; almost one snow scooter per person is registered. With these snow scooters the residents can make tracks to hitherto inaccessible parts of the countryside. Tourists, too, can hire snow vehicles; it's wise to go with a guide. But it's forbidden to go hunting with snowmobiles. Otherwise, hunting—and the outdoors in general—is a good incentive to attract settlers.

Town Centre

The best way to see how the citizens live is to visit the big, cheerful country store in the centre of town. Here the locals stock up on kitchenware, fresh fruit, thermal underwear and TV sets (yes, there is a local TV station for those long winter nights). Everything seems abundantly supplied in the store, but the *akevitt* and all other types of liquor are rationed to one bottle per adult per fortnight. For tourists the shopping opportunities tend towards postcards picturing local attractions, Svalbard T-shirts and souvenirs of the type found on the mainland. Next to the store stands another reassuring link with the outside world —a bank. It's open from 10 a.m. to 4 p.m., if you'd like to cash a traveller's cheque in an unusual part of the world.

Near the centre of town, if you look beyond the road carefully you'll probably see wild flowers, pale arctic survivors. Do not pick the flowers as they are lovingly conserved, in view of their obvious scarcity.

One of the few places you'll see grass on the otherwise stony ground is in the cemetery, where simple white crosses stand out against the unaccustomed patches of green.

As in any Norwegian village there is a church. This one is unusually cosy and attractive, with a pine-panelled interior and a pale modern altar painting. The Evangelical Lutheran Church is the official, state-supported church of Norway; the law requires the King and at least half of the cabinet to be church members. Other local institutions include the hospital, the small "Polar University", a school, a brass band, a national dance ensemble and an athletic club.

Longyearbyen Museum

The museum opened in 1981 in a building which once housed 140 pigs. It operates daily from mid-May to mid-September and every second Sunday in winter. When the cruise ships arrive, volunteer guides stand by to answer questions in several languages. Look at the paintings in the outer hall—a frieze in eight parts by a miner named Martin Barlund, dated 1956. Many of the items inside illustrate the harsh life of Spitsbergen hunters and fishermen: home-made harpoons, trappers' diaries, a guitar one pioneer built from scraps of metal and wood to while away the long night. There are "souvenirs" of the fighting on Spitsbergen during World War II, and documents on the polar expeditions that passed through. Don't miss the photos of the Spanish team that flew to Longyearbyen in 1982, intending to reach the North Pole by motorbikes. The bikes froze, the sledges balked, and the "explorers" barely got beyond the airport.

A much more elaborate—and successful— operation, the Transglobe expedition led by Sir Ranulph Twisleton-Wykeham Fiennes, also passed through Longyearbyen. In the summer of 1982 the group's 12,000-ton support ship, the *Benjamin Bowring,* became a familiar sight in the Adventfjord as Fiennes and his companion, Charles Burton, intrepidly snowmobiled towards the North Pole. When they finally arrived at Greenwich they were greatly acclaimed as the first travellers to circumnavigate the globe via the poles.

Barentsburg

The Russian mining town of Barentsburg is about 40 km (25 miles) southwest of Longyearbyen. The town is named after the 16th-century Dutch explorer Willem Barents, who gave Spitsbergen its name.

From the fjord, the plan of Barentsburg may be seen to be more organized, less haphazard, than the capitalist enclave of Longyearbyen. On the outskirts are cattle barns and greenhouses: the settlers have to strive for self-sufficiency. The long, straight main street is lined with utilitarian, low-rise Russian apartment houses as well as some smaller, more colourful buildings.

A coal ship may be standing by in the harbour, but little activity is visible. Russian coal production at Barentsburg and at Pyramiden, 80 km (50 miles) to the northeast, is said to total far less than the Norwegian output on the island. Moreover, the withdrawal of financial support by the Russian government puts the whole future of the Russian presence on Spitsbergen in doubt. No roads connect the Russian settlement to Longyearbyen, and there is little contact between the Russian and Norwegian communities. But tour companies can arrange visits by boat, snowmobile or helicopter, depending on the time of year.

FOSSILS

Tourists coming ashore at Longyearbyen are met by local schoolchildren selling the Spitsbergen equivalent of quaint native souvenirs. The youngsters set up shop on a packing crate, laying out a dozen fossils for sale; many more are squirreled away in reserve. The shy, young vendors may claim their trophies are 100 million or 300 million years old. Whatever their true age, embedded within are fascinating remains of prehistoric shellfish, plants or insects.

Some fossils only 50 million years old contain evidence—twigs and leaves—that forests of the kind of trees now common in Europe once grew on Spitsbergen. Another proof that Svalbard once was timberland: the coal mines. Hundreds of thousands of tons of coal used to be dug up in Spitsbergen every year. The shallow horizontal seams of coal are, of course, the fossilized remains of all those trees. Incidentally, the fact that the earth around the mine shafts is permanently deep-frozen makes life considerably less dangerous for miners in Spitsbergen compared with other areas.

Coal was the economic base for settlement on Svalbard since the turn of the century. But the Russian and Ukrainian population is now declining and the Norwegians have cut production too, as demand has fallen and much cheaper coal is available from other sources. Norwegian subsidies to Svalbard continue, however, with an eye to the rich fishing grounds, and the possibility of oil discoveries.

CULTURAL NOTES

Bjørnstjerne Bjørnson (1832–1910) The winner of the Nobel Prize for literature in 1903, Bjørnson was one of the towering figures in the years that led up to Norway's independence. Poet, playwright, campaigning journalist and orator, as a young man he succeeded Ibsen as artistic director of the Bergen Theatre. He stimulated Norwegian national pride: his poem *Ja, vi elsker dette landet* ("Yes, we love this land") became the national anthem. He lived at the head of Langfjorden near Molde for many years, writing his tales of peasant life. His three-page essay on laziness inspired many a student: on page one he wrote "This"; on page two, "is"; and on page three, "laziness".

Edvard Grieg (1843–1907) Almost single-handedly, Grieg put Norwegian music on the map. Two of his works, the *Piano Concerto* and the Suite from *Peer Gynt*, written for Ibsen's play, regularly feature in choices of the world's favourite classics. He studied in Germany, but returned and fell under the spell of his country's folk tunes and rhythms. Unlike many composers, he was recognized when still young (Liszt praised the *Piano Concerto*, written when Grieg was only 24), and was paid a generous state salary from the age of 31. In 1885 he bought the Troldhaugen estate near Bergen, the city of his birth. A fine pianist, he undertook concert tours all over Europe, in spite of ill health.

Knut Hamsun (1859–1952) Like the heroes of his novels, Knut Hamsun swam against the tide, attacking the social realism of late 19th-century literature and such writers as Ibsen and Tolstoy. He grew up in the Arctic, on the Lofoten Islands, and worked for years as a labourer, including a spell in the United States as a farmhand and a Chicago streetcar conductor. Hamsun's characters are strange, combative, irrational and self-sufficient. *Hunger* (1899) is the story of a starving young writer; in *Growth of the Soil* (1920) a peasant battles with nature to build a life on a remote farm. Hamsun was awarded the Nobel Prize for literature in 1920. Late in life, he was alone among major Norwegian writers in supporting Nazi Germany, even in its occupation of Norway. After the war, he was imprisoned on a charge of treason, but freed because of his age.

Henrik Ibsen (1828–1906) More than any other writer, Ibsen changed the nature of modern

85

European drama. His realistic but heavily symbolic plays, with their psychological insights and clear diamond-hard prose, often shocked his contemporaries. With *A Doll's House*, *Ghosts* and *An Enemy of the People* he set off violent debates among the critics, but his technical mastery, gained from years working in the theatre, was undisputed.

Bitter experience fuelled his creative fire. While Ibsen was still a young child his father went bankrupt, reducing the family from prosperity to penury. He was packed off at 15 from his home town, Skien, in the south, to another small town to be a pharmacist's apprentice; his first play was written in his spare time. Moving to Christiania (Oslo) to study, he managed to have a play performed and then to get a job in the new theatre in Bergen. Shy and withdrawn, he found directing a torture, and his own early plays were failures. Back in Christiania at the Norwegian Theatre he found himself having to direct farces to attract audiences, but the theatre went bust anyway. Ibsen spent the next 27 years abroad, in Rome, Dresden and Munich, and it was by leaving Norway that he at last achieved recognition, with *Brand* and *Peer Gynt*, both of them attacks on Norwegian narrow-mindedness and provincialism. He returned to his homeland in 1891, fresh from the success of *Hedda Gabler*. *The Master Builder* and *John Gabriel Borkman* followed, confirming Henrik Ibsen as one of the world's greatest dramatists.

Alexander Kielland (1849–1906) While Bjørnson loved the mountains, they only irritated Kielland, who drew the curtains of his house in Molde to hide them every day he was governor of Romsdal. He turned to the sea, and spent hours at Bud on the shores of the turbulent Hustadvika, watching the waves. Born to a prosperous Stavanger family, he studied law and ran the family factory, but became a committed social reformer, attacking the bureaucracy and the established church through the medium of his witty novels and short stories.

Edvard Munch (1863–1944) One of the greatest revolutionaries in the history of art, Munch was a tortured genius who painted some of the most memorable images ever created: *The Scream*, *The Vampire*, *The Sick Child*, *Jealousy*. His explorations of violent colour and distortion of line pointed the way to the Expressionism of Matisse, Kokoschka and Nolde. Few artists have ever revealed their own mental anguish so nakedly. The neurotic emotionalism which pervades his work had its roots in a tragic childhood. Munch's mother died of tuberculosis when he was only five. Ten years later his eldest sister died of the same disease and another sister suffered from mental illness. Death and sickness became persistent themes in his pictures. Reflecting his tortured feelings, women are portrayed as virginal, or brazenly sexual, or terrifying, sometimes all in the same painting. Munch suffered a mental breakdown himself in 1908, a catharsis after which he returned to Norway and painted in a far more positive frame of mind, revelling in the joys of nature. He continued to work at an energetic pace until the end of his life, dying in Oslo during the occupation. He left his vast collection to the city, which built the Munch Museum to house it.

The Sami People. Scandinavia's northern tribe prefer to be called *Sami* (sometimes written *Same*), rather than Lapps, a word that is derogatory. Anthropologists cannot say for certain where they came from, or the route they took; some similarities of physical feature and language suggest a link with the Samoyeds of northern Siberia. Today there are between 50,000 and 100,000 Sami, depending how the descendants of intermarriage are counted. More than half live in Norway, the rest in Finland, Sweden and on the Kola peninsula in Russia.

Many of Norway's Sami have settled down in villages and live like other Norwegians, but some 3,000 still follow the traditional nomadic life of reindeer-herding. About 200,000 of the semi-wild animals are kept on the plains near the Finnish-Norwegian border. Wonderfully adapted to the winter, they live on moss and lichens which they find under the snow. In summer, many are marched north to the coast to graze on the grass that appears as the snow thaws, while their owners live in turf huts or reindeer-skin tents (also to be seen all over the north in the form of souvenir stalls to tempt summer visitors). The radioactive fallout from the nuclear disaster at Chernobyl in 1986 caused appalling long-term problems, contaminating the lichens and thus the reindeer meat, making it unfit for human consumption.

The Sami language, or languages—there are several distinct forms—have equal status with Norwegian in the northern counties. People who register as Sami can vote in elections of the Sami parliament which meets in Karasjok, a small town near the Finnish border and the Sami capital. Spring sees a flurry of activity there: it's the traditional time for weddings, reindeer races and folk music performances.

Shopping

Norway is known for silver and pewter ware, ceramics and glass, worked in imaginative modern designs as well as revivals of Viking and medieval motifs. Polished specimens of semi-precious minerals have an eye-catching beauty. The country can supply any kind of gear for the outdoor life: sailing, fishing, hiking or camping. Although prices are high by international standards, you can at least recover the sales tax.

Where?

Many towns have a Husfliden craft store run by the Norwegian Association for Home Arts and Crafts, worth a visit to see a selection of high-quality crafts. Also try the department stores, jewellers, museum shops and specialist shops for clothing and sports equipment.

Books

Norwegians are great readers—the long winter evenings may be one reason. Every town has at least one good bookstore, with English, German and French sections as well as Norwegian, so there's no problem if you run short of holiday reading.

Ceramics and Glass

Potters produce unlimited numbers of mugs, plates and candlesticks, but this too is an art form in Scandinavia, with a wealth of useful and ornamental ceramics.

Norwegian glass traditionally had a grey tint, a tone still seen in rustic glass and many modern designs. Now all colours are used, for drinking glasses and bowls, glass animals and birds.

Foods

Some of the local delicacies such as smoked salmon and *gravlaks* (cured salmon) are sold in sealed packs ready to carry home. Other long-life products are marinated herring in jars, red "kaviar" (fish paste) in tubes and various cheeses including *geitost,* the caramel-coloured goat's cheese which you'll have either come to love or loathe during your visit. The cheese slicers used to cut it—you see them on the *koldtbord* buffet—make a useful souvenir. The design was invented by a Norwegian in 1925, not as an economy measure but because this and some other cheeses taste better in thin slices.

Furs and Skins

It may be a controversial issue in other countries, but in Norway practicality and tradition combine to keep animal furs and skins in widespread use. If you have qualms, Norwegians will point out that reindeer are domesticated and using their skins is no different from making shoes from leather. And on the luxury level, almost all arctic fox and mink fur comes from farmed animals, with strict controls to ensure humane treatment.

Woollens and textiles

Knitted gloves, hats and ski-caps, scarves, sweaters and jackets come in bold colours and patterns to brighten a winter's day, or in the subtle shades of natural wool. A practical souvenir of Norway, they could be pressed into service during your trip if you arrive unprepared for a cold spell. Lighter versions are made in cotton. Other textile specialities are woven rugs and wall-hangings, embroidered table linen and regional folk costumes. If you can't see yourself in an elaborately embroidered blouse, charming children's versions are available.

Silver and Pewter

The rich veins of pure silver found at Kongsberg have long since been exhausted but the tradition remains of fine silver jewellery and tableware. Look for enamelled silver bracelets and brooches.

Pewter was once a modest substitute for silver; now it is a respected medium in its own right. Norwegian pewter is lead-free, so you need not be concerned when using it to hold or serve food.

Sports and Camping Equipment

Essentials and accessories for skiing, camping and sailing may not be bargains, but you will be assured of good quality. Norwegian rucksacks in particular are world-renowned. So are boots for walking and climbing, winter clothing and sailors' oilskins. Look for locally made hunting knives, but don't try to take them on an aircraft in your hand baggage. Fishing equipment, from a child's first rod to a deep-sea trawler's gear, is the best.

Woodcarvings

Some of the most attractive souvenirs are cheerful painted figures of fishermen, reindeer, birds, boxes, model fishing boats or Viking ships. And of course trolls, the gnomes of Norse mythology, turn up in all shapes and sizes. These carvings can be true works of art, sculptures of Norway's wildlife or imaginative abstract designs.

Dining Out

In the past, Norwegians always had to be self-sufficient and menus still make good use of local produce. As you would expect from one of the world's leading fishing nations, the fish is superb, from fresh cod and pickled herring to the abundant salmon. Reindeer and cloudberries give the food an Arctic accent.

Breakfast

Usually a serve-yourself affair, breakfast can consist of a small selection of fruits, cheeses, cereals, breads and crispbreads (*knekkebrød*), perhaps with boiled eggs. But some hotels offer a much larger buffet with herring in various sauces, salads, ham and salami.

Lunch

The *koldtbord*, or cold table, is a lunchtime buffet featured at larger hotels and on the ships of the Coastal Express. It's usual to make several visits, taking a fresh plate each time. The first might be a choice of fish and seafood: crab, prawns, herring (*sild*), marinated and perhaps in a salad, cured salmon (*gravlaks*) or a whole baked salmon (*laks*) or seatrout (*sjøørret*). Then come the cold meats, pâtés and salads. Usually—in spite of the name—there are hot dishes too: fish, chicken, pork, roasts and stews, vegetables and potatoes. And then follow cheeses, fruit and desserts, both pastries and old-fashioned puddings.

Local people usually have a more modest lunch, often that contradiction in terms, the open sandwich or *smørbrød*. The Norwegian language actually has a word for the toppings, *pålegg*, meaning "something to put on bread". Among the options are shrimps, ham, roast beef, smoked salmon and assorted salads.

Dinner

Traditionally, quite simple dishes are served at the evening meal. Fish is poached or sautéed in butter. Meats include excellent local lamb, as a roast or in a traditional dish called *fårikål* (lamb or mutton stewed with cabbage and black pepper). Meat balls (*kjøttkaker*) are a staple, made from beef or pork. Reindeer comes as steaks or smoked and thinly sliced: lean, tender and tasty.

Cheeses

The typically Norwegian goats' milk cheese, *geitost*, is caramel-coloured and sweet, and generally eaten in the form of thin slices produced by a special cutter. This "brown cheese", a favourite of homesick Norwegians, was originally an economical way of using up the whey left over after cheesemaking. It was boiled until it reduced to a chocolate brown sticky substance, and eaten spread on bread. An ingenious dairymaid had the idea of mixing in cream to make it more palatable. Today, tens of thousands of tonnes of *geitost* are produced in big dairies, but many people insist on the original made in the old way in a handful of villages in Gudbrandsdal, east of Ålesund.

Gammelost is a matured, strong cheese; if you want something milder, the local versions of French, Swiss and Dutch cheeses are often very good.

Desserts

Summer fruits make delicious desserts, especially the intensely flavoured local raspberries and the scented wild cloudberries *(multer)*. Gathering them is a treasured tradition and the best areas are well-kept secrets. Blueberries and sharp-tasting lin-

CURE ALL

Until a few decades ago, Norwegians had to ensure their winter food supplies by preserving seasonal surpluses. Methods included salting, drying, pickling or otherwise curing, all processes that tend to concentrate flavours or add to them. People acquired a taste for these foods that remains to this day—many of them prefer rehydrated dried cod to fish that comes fresh from the sea. *Spekemat* is the generic term for cured food: *spekepølse* is a cured sausage rather like salami, *spekeskinke* is cured ham; and smoked and dried mutton is known as *fenalår*. All these might be served as appetizers with *flatbrød*, hard baked thin bread (another example of a food that will keep).

Norway exports more dried and salt cod than all other countries added together, and still keeps some for herself. Dried cod softened with caustic soda solution for two days, and washed for two more, becomes *lutefisk*. Glutinous and strongly flavoured, it's served poached as a traditional winter treat. Smoked salmon is now one of the world's favourite foods but *gravlaks*, salmon seasoned with fresh dill, salt, pepper and sugar and pressed under a weight, is fast catching up.

Racks of cod hung out to dry: it may end up in Portugal as **bacalhau**.

gonberries are two more targets of the keen-eyed pickers.

Desserts often include plenty of whipped cream, as in *tilslørte bondepiker* ("veiled farmgirls"), comprising layers of stewed apple, biscuit crumbs and cream. Sponge cake topped with apple is another favourite, and pancakes are popular.

Drinks

All the usual drinks are available but expensive, and you'll see many local people sticking to water. The tap water is good and pure; bottled mineral waters include Farris from a famous spring near Larvik.

Strict rules against drinking and driving, as well as the prices, mean that many Norwegians think of alcoholic drinks as something for a special occasion. Then they can let their hair down—and take a taxi home.

Beer *(øl)* comes in various strengths including low- and no-alcohol versions. The national firewater *akevitt*, distilled from potatoes or grain, is served cold, sometimes with beer chasers and flaked dried cod as a snack.

Wines are considered something of a luxury. Prices are quite high and the selection tends to be limited; imports are in the hands of a state monopoly.

Sports

The scenery of lakes, mountains and fjords combined with long summer days makes the country a paradise for outdoor pursuits: hiking, horseriding, canoeing and sailing. There is excellent fishing for trout and salmon in the rivers, and for sea fish in the fjords and around the offshore islands. Bird-watchers can log a multitude of species, especially of seabirds in the vast colonies found on rocky islets and cliffs along the west and north coasts. Among spectator sports, soccer rates as a national religion.

Sailing

Most Norwegians are ambitious to own their own boat, for these descendants of the Vikings like nothing better than getting on to the water and heading up a fjord or out to a deserted island. If you would like to join them, you will find boats for hire at campsites, hotels, lakeside villages and harbours all along the coast. Some resorts have sailing schools. Wind-surfing has taken off, as everywhere else round Europe's coasts, but here the cold water makes wetsuits essential.

Hidden rocks and strong currents make these waters potentially dangerous, even more so for strangers. Anyone planning to navigate the rugged coastline will need to obtain up-to-date charts, and the law states that lifejackets must be provided for everyone aboard.

Canoeing and Rafting

Lakes, rivers and fjords make Norway a prime destination for kayaking; canoes are rented out at many campsites and holiday hotels. Tour operators offer white-water rafting down the rapids of some fast-flowing rivers.

Swimming

Yes, you may be able to swim in the sea! The water sometimes warms up enough to make it bearable, especially from sheltered beaches in the south. Hardy souls even proclaim it a pleasure to swim in the Arctic, notably around the Lofoten Islands where the Gulf Stream still exerts an influence, keeping summer sea temperatures marginally above that of ice water. Waterskiing is well-suited to sheltered fjords, and scuba-diving clubs organize classes and expeditions.

Larger hotels and leisure centres have heated pools and a lot of towns have indoor "waterworlds" with wave machines and slides—and guaranteed warmth.

Fishing

With so many lakes and streams, and a vast length of coastline, fishing is a favourite pastime as well as a great traditional industry. Stocks are still good, although acid rain has damaged many freshwater habitats.

Anyone over 16 fishing the lakes and rivers must have a national permit (available from post offices) *and* a local licence, sold at tourist offices, hotels and campsites. Fishing in the sea or fjords is free of charge. The Norwegian Tourist Board publishes a useful book, *Angling in Norway*, with information on the rules, species and locations.

Bird-Watching

From Runde, a great rock standing out of the sea southwest of Ålesund, to the northern tip of Norway, a chain of bird sanctuaries has been established to protect the seabirds. Some of the biggest colonies are on the Lofoten Islands where you should see puffins, kittiwakes, guillemots and dozens of other species. Little arctic terns that migrate all the way from the Antarctic defend their nests against marauding skuas and herring gulls; gannets and fulmars skim the waves ready to grab a fish.

Fedje, an island near Bergen, claims 225 recorded species, which include rarities blown off course in storms. Utsira near Haugesund caps that with 296.

Hiking and Mountaineering

Mountain tracks, high plains and idyllic valleys make ideal walking country, and with Norway's "right to-roam" tradition you are free to go anywhere—as long as you don't cause damage. You can carry your own tent or stay in hostels or mountain cabins scattered across all the popular hiking areas—they mostly open from June to mid-September.

Winter Sports

Skiing, especially cross-country skiing, is a sport that Norway regards as its own, saying "We allow other countries to win now and then; otherwise they would give up and we would have nobody to compete against!" Alpine skiing flourishes too, and the newer sport of snow-boarding. The season lasts until April in the main resorts such as Lillehammer and Geilo, and later as you go further north. In fact, it's possible to ski right through summer in the north and on high glaciers; the sight of someone skiing in bikini or shorts is not unusual.

The Hard Facts

Airports

Oslo's Gardermoen airport lies 53 km (33 miles) northeast of the city centre. Airport buses leave from the terminal behind the Central Railway Station; travel time is 50 min. The airport train runs four times an hour from Oslo Central Station; the ride takes 33 min. Bergen Airport, Flesland is 19 km (12 miles) southwest of the city. Airport buses run to and from the terminal at the City Bus Station and take about 30 min.

Both Oslo and Bergen airports have duty-free shops, banks, bars, restaurants and cafeterias, car rental and information desks.

Stavanger and Kristiansand airports also have direct flights to several European cities. Over 50 other cities and towns are served by a comprehensive domestic network, including Trondheim, Bodø, Tromsø (with flights to Svalbard) and Kirkenes.

Car Rental

Hiring a car is an expensive but convenient way of getting around in summer (winter driving is best left to the local experts). Some of the big international rental companies are represented in Norway, but to get the best deal it may be worth making a reservation through one of them in your home country, before your visit. Good local companies also operate from airports and main cities, but whichever you use, check that rates include full insurance against loss and damage, and local taxes. There is usually no limit on the distance you can cover, but an extra charge may be levied for drop-off at a different location, and for additional driver(s).

To rent a car, you need to be over 21 (25 with some companies) and in possession of a valid driving licence. You are expected to pay with a major credit card.

Climate

The key word is unpredictable. The average daytime temperature in Oslo in summer is 18°C (64°F), in Tromsø 12°C (54°F), but such figures conceal large variations. It may be baking hot, even—though rarely—in the Arctic, or cold and wet. Summers in any case are short, lasting from mid-June to mid-August. That means that spring is late and autumn comes early, although both can be beautiful times for a visit.

Winter sports fans usually find no shortage of snow in the mountain resorts, lasting well into May (longer in the north) and may enjoy a run of clear sunny days.

Clothing

Take a raincoat, and a rain hat or umbrella. If you are going to the Arctic, take a warm, weather-proof jacket with a hood (or a hat) and gloves. Strong, comfortable walking shoes or boots are essential for shore excursions and hikes. In summer, be prepared for hot days too.

Some restaurants in the big cities ask men to wear a jacket and tie, otherwise Norwegians are quite informal. Beachwear is fashionable and often minimal when the weather permits. Most southern coastal towns have a nudist beach.

Communications

The telephone system is modern and works well. Norway's country code is 47. There are no area codes. To make an international call from Norway, dial 00 and then the country code (1 for US and Canada, 44 for UK), area code (omitting initial zero, if any) and number. There are plenty of coin- and card-operated phones; cards can be bought from post offices and Narvesen kiosks. You can also call from telephone offices in larger towns.

Mobile phones have rapidly become indispensable to Norwegians on land and offshore.

It generally costs much more to use the phone in your hotel room, unless you use one of the calling cards issued by international telephone companies. Fax messages can be sent and received through many hotels, major post offices and business service bureaux.

Postal services are good, although quite slow from remote locations. Airmail reaches most European destinations in 3 to 5 days. Stamps are usually available wherever postcards are on sale, as well as at post offices.

Crime

Norway is one of the world's safest countries, but street crime, formerly unknown, has been on the increase in the cities, fuelled as in most places by a growing drug problem. Just take normal precautions: avoid dark or lonely places at night, and don't leave anything desirable on show when parking your car.

Driving

The short sections of divided highway are mainly confined to the vicinity of Oslo. Elsewhere, major roads are paved; secondary roads are gravel surfaced. Many mountain routes are closed in winter but most others, even in the Arctic, are efficiently cleared.

In mountain and fjord country—the greater part of Norway

in fact—roads are narrow, tortuous and busy in summer, and a journey up the west coast entails more time on ferries than on the road. The scenery may be beautiful, but progress is inevitably slow.

Road information is available from Norges Automobil-Forbund Information Centre in Oslo, tel. 22 34 14 00, or Oslo Tourist Office, tel. 22 33 43 86.

Speed limits are 50 kph (31 mph) in towns, 80 kph (50 mph) out of town and 90 kph (56 mph) on highways *(motorveier)*, unless other limits are posted. Low-beam headlights are mandatory during daylight. Drivers and passengers must wear seat belts; children under 7 must be correctly strapped in. A red warning triangle, first aid kit and spare bulbs for the lights should be carried in the vehicle.

Laws against driving under the influence of alcohol or drugs are strict, and rigorously enforced. The alcohol limit is the equivalent of one *small* drink; to exceed it is to risk a prison sentence. Fines for motoring offences may be levied on the spot. Not all petrol (gas) stations accept credit cards.

Drivers entering Oslo, Bergen and Trondheim must pay a toll, and there are tolls for ferries and some major highways and many bridges.

Emergencies

To call the Police dial 112; the Fire Service 110; an Ambulance 113.

Essentials

Be sure to take sunscreen cream, even in winter if you are going to ski (and a high protection factor is recommended, as ozone depletion in the upper atmosphere increases levels of ultra-violet), dark glasses, binoculars, film and any medicines you may need—the same brands may not be available. Insect repellent is essential in summer and autumn (Arctic mosquitoes are notorious) but effective products are available locally.

Most people, including returning residents, take in their full duty-free drink allowance; prices in Norway are high.

Etiquette

Norwegians are exceptionally courteous; the older generation are particularly formal and polite. They are on time for appointments, and dress quite formally for business meetings. It's usual to shake hands when meeting people, and when taking leave of them.

Formalities

Visas are not needed by travellers from western European countries, Canada and Australia. US citizens may stay for up to three months total in the Nordic countries (Norway, Sweden, Denmark, Finland and Iceland) without a visa.

There is no limit on the amount of local and foreign currency that may be imported.

Residents of European countries may take the following into Norway duty-free: 200 cigarettes or 250 g tobacco; 1 litre of spirits and 1 litre of wine **or** 2 litres of wine and 2 litres of beer; a small amount of perfume and eau de cologne. Residents of non-European countries may import 400 cigarettes or 500 g tobacco products, 1 litre spirits and 1 litre wine **or** 2 litres wine and 2 litres beer; 50 g perfume and 1/2 litre eau de cologne. You must be aged 20 or more to import alcoholic drinks, 18 or more for tobacco products.

Health and Medical Matters

In summer in the Arctic, use a sunscreen with a high protection factor (at least 15) and make sure that children do the same.

Pharmacies sell a wide variety of medications, but some will be under unfamiliar names.

It is advisable to take out comprehensive travel insurance, including coverage of medical expenses. Citizens of most western European countries can get free emergency treatment; it helps if they carry a qualifying document, for UK citizens the Form E111 obtainable from post offices before leaving home. Keep receipts for any payments you have to make, in order to claim refunds.

Language

Norwegian comes in two distinct forms: the formal *bokmål* derived from the official language used when Denmark ruled Norway, and a contrived blend of regional dialects called *nynorsk* ("new Norwegian"). Fortunately they are similar enough for one to be understood by habitual users of the other. The alphabet has three more letters than English: æ, ø and å. They follow in that order after the z in dictionaries and telephone directories.

English is quite widely understood, especially by young people who all study it in school and by anyone who has to deal with visitors.

Media

State-run TV channels are augmented in many hotels by satellite and cable channels, including BBC World, Sky News, CNN and various European channels. Reception of BBC World Service, Voice of America and other English-language radio stations is good on short wave, especially in the evening and early morning.

Newspapers and magazines in English are widely available. The 99

UK and other major European newspapers arrive in the main cities by early evening on the day of publication.

Money

The currency is the *krone* (NOK or kr), divided into 100 *øre*. Banknotes range from kr 50 to 1,000; coins from 50 øre to kr 20.

Foreign currency and traveller's cheques may be changed at banks, exchange offices, large post offices and the bigger hotels (at a poorer rate). Major credit cards are very widely accepted in shops, hotels and restaurants. Using them or bank cards, cash may be obtained from automatic distributors (ATMs), if you know the PIN (personal identification number).

Opening Hours

Museums and other attractions generally open from 9.30 or 10 a.m. to about 4 p.m. Some close on Monday. It is worth trying to find out in advance.

Shops open Monday to Friday 9 a.m.–4 or 5 p.m. (late closing Thursdays, 6 or 7 p.m.), and Saturdays 9 or 10 a.m.–1 or 3 p.m.

Post offices open Monday to Friday 8 or 8.30 a.m.–4 or 5 p.m., Saturdays 8 a.m.–1 p.m.

Banks generally open Monday to Friday 8.15 a.m.–3 p.m. (to 3.30 p.m. in winter); late closing Thursdays, 5 p.m.).

Photography and Video

Colour print film and transparency film are widely available. Colour prints can be quickly processed locally but transparency film is best taken back to your own country for processing.

Video-tape is available. Pre-recorded tapes are compatible with most of Europe, but not the US.

Public Holidays

January 1	New Year's Day
May 1	Labour Day
May 8	Liberation Day
May 17	National Day
December 25,26	Christmas

March/April: Maundy Thursday, Good Friday, Easter Monday; May/June: Ascension Day, Whit Monday

Public Transport

Within the bigger cities, purchase of a tourist card gives free bus and tram travel for a specified number of days. The Oslo Card *(Oslo Kort)* is the most useful of these, giving 1 to 3 days of travel on trams, buses, the subway and trains within greater Oslo as well as admission to most museums, car parking in city-run parks and discounts on theatre and concert tickets and some tours.

Taxis are readily available but expensive. Trains link Oslo to Stockholm and Gothenburg in Sweden; to Stavanger; to Bergen (a tourist train offers a commentary in English); and to Bodø in the Arctic, via Trondheim. And where the trains stop, buses continue. Regular domestic flights connect 50 airports, many of them quite small.

Tax Refund

A sales tax, called *merverdiavgift* or *moms* for short, is applied to almost all goods and services. But you can escape paying the tax (as much as 23%) on larger purchases, unless you are resident in Norway, Sweden, Denmark or Finland. Look for a store or shop displaying a "Tax-Free for Tourists" logo; that includes most craft, clothing and the larger souvenir shops, and all department stores. Ask for a Tax-Free Shopping Cheque whenever you spend more than the minimum amount to qualify. You will need to show your passport or other proof of residence.

Write your name and home address on the cheques. When you leave Norway, at ports, airports and land borders, or on a cruise ship or ferry, cash them at the Tax Refund desk.

Time

Norway is on GMT + 1, advancing to GMT + 2 for summer time between April and October. Thus it is one hour ahead of UK and Ireland.

Tipping

A service charge is included in restaurant bills, but an extra 5 to 10% can be added for especially good service. Porters are tipped 5 krone per bag. Taxi fares may be rounded up by a small amount.

Toilets

Clean public lavatories are provided at rail and main bus stations, department stores and some tourist sites.

Tourist Information

All major towns have a Tourist Information Office, generally open from 9 a.m. to 4 p.m., Monday to Saturday. Most of them have excellent information leaflets and maps of the local area. Many of the offices in smaller or more remote places are open in summer only.

Voltage

The electrical supply is 220V, 50 Hz, AC. Plugs are of the mainland European type, with two round pins. Apart from shavers for which a marked outlet is provided, any 110V equipment needs a transformer as well as an adaptor.

Water

Tap water is safe to drink everywhere in Norway, although some people prefer bottled mineral water.

INDEX

GENERAL EDITOR:
Barbara Ender-Jones
EDITOR:
Alice Taucher
LAYOUT:
Luc Malherbe
PHOTO CREDITS:
Laurence Carducci, p. 2;
Hémisphères/Wysocki;
Hémisphères/Soumillard;
Hémisphères/Boisvieux;
Peter Tonn, p. 14;
Walter Imber,
pp. 22, 75, 76, 81
MAPS:
Elsner & Schichor;
Huber Kartographie

Copyright © 2001, 2000
by JPM Publications S.A.
12, avenue William-Fraisse,
1006 Lausanne, Switzerland
information@jpmguides.com
http://www.jpmguides.com/

Printed in Switzerland
Weber/Bienne (CTP)

BERGEN